VALUE INNOVA

Value Innovation Works

Move Mountains ......Drive sustainable, profitable growth!

Deliver Exceptional Value to the Most Important Customers in Your Value Chains

A "How To" Guide

Richard K. Lee

Nina E. Goodrich

VALUE INNOVATION WORKS

ISBN:-10: 1470020572
ISBN-13: 978 1470020576

TESTIMONIALS

The insights and inspiration of Richard ("Dick") K. Lee's Value Innovation Process provided an essential foundation for our organization's first foray into new product development. As a result, Compassion has launched two new fundraising products in the past 18 months that have enabled 115,000 families to have clean water in their homes, 180 child development centers to launch and over 25,000 new donors to join in the fight to free children around the world from extreme poverty. These elegantly simple methods make true innovation accessible to all kinds of organizations!

Ed Cleaver, Senior Director USA Product Marketing Division,
Compassion International
Colorado Springs, CO
USA

Value Innovation Works is no Management for Dummies puff piece. It is a thorough and compelling blueprint for consistently implementing innovation that is effective and profitable. Dick Lee and Nina Goodrich have used their extensive industrial experience to highlight tools and techniques proven to get real results. The book is distinctly actionable and superbly readable. You and your firm's leadership team won't fail to visualize how these powerful tools can energize your own innovation engine. Value innovation really does work and this book shows you how to put it to work for your company.

Thomas A. Dillon, Former Senior Group VP, SAIC
San Diego, CA
USA

"If you are looking to make a great impact, the Value Innovation Process is the best way to develop killer business strategies. The Value Innovation Process is not for the timid, it requires you to challenge much of your organization's prior thinking.

Repeatable, successful Value Innovation is the goal we should all share. Richard K. Lee's approach is to teach that innovation itself is an important science to be learned.

All VCs, angel investors and equity investors will benefit by using the Value Innovation Process as a key part of their due diligence activities, their investment success rates will go up!

Value Innovation is the critical component in growing the economic pie. The better we become at such innovation processes the more we all benefit."

Brad Fehn, Managing Partner, Duart Capital LLC
interim CEO, FoldedPak, Inc.
Denver, CO
USA

"The Value Innovations Process helped us to identify the specific individuals within the target customers' organization who are our Most Important Customers (MIC's) and to focus on developing compelling value propositions that meet their articulated and unarticulated requirements.

We implemented the Value Innovation Process (VIP) across multifunctional product development teams. The use of the VIP allowed these teams to develop a common language, and deeper, richer insights into the customers' requirements that resulted in a tighter alignment on the customers' needs and faster product definition."

Mark Forrest, GM Field Service Division, Trimble Navigation
Former COO and GM, Caterpillar Trimble Control Technologies
Westminster, CO
USA

I spent six years with Pure Insight observing, measuring, and reporting on the effectiveness of front end of innovation tools and methodologies. I have whiled away many hours at conferences listening to tales of great leaps in product performance via one school of thought or another. But many times I would find myself asking 'is that how it really happened? Or maybe are you post rationalising a happy set of coincidences'. Even more often 'could you do it again and again?' and 'how can I take what you have told me and apply it in my business to be successful?'

Value Innovation is the only methodology I have looked into which delivers on all of these counts again and again and I recommend this book it to you wholeheartedly for that reason.

Jane Hogan, Managing Director, TwentyEightManagement
Durham, England

"Often technology drives new product development with mixed business results. AstenJohnson now employs the Value Innovation Process to get it right. The Value Innovation Process provides an effective toolset to determine our customers unmet needs. Consequently we are better targeting growth opportunities in a tough market, and changing the way our product developers think and work."

Graham Jackson, Vice President - Business Leader, Advanced Products, AstenJohnson
Kanata, ON
Canada

Value Innovation Works picks up where the innovation guru's books leave off. This book gives the innovation practitioner a 10-Step Value Innovation Process roadmap with a rich enabling toolbox to get right down to work on innovation. Value Innovation Works provides wonderful examples of these tools in action and an amazing array of very practical insights. I've used the Value Innovation Process and it Works, very well! Follow it and you'll be able to move mountains.

Bruce Janda, Global Innovation Leader – Forming, AstenJohnson
Appleton, WI
USA

"More and more now being operationally excellent is no longer the complete answer. I see Richard K. Lee's Value Innovation Process as a breakthrough approach to Delight your customer rather than just satisfy them."

Gary Keatings, Vice President Solutions Design EMEA, DHL
Glasgow, Scotland

One phrase to describe Richard ("Dick) K. Lee - "the consummate innovation expert". I met Dick at O'hare International Airport on board a flight from Chicago to Denver. During the duration of the flight Dick passionately shared his insights on Value Innovation, and how companies could leverage it to accelerate growth and profits by delivering exceptional value to their most important customers in their value chains. It was something that seemed pretty obvious however, rather complicated since most companies struggle to meet this basic expectation. Seeking to better understand how companies could accomplish this order, my curiosity led me to attend Dick's flagship workshop - "Mastering Value Innovation". In this workshop the lights went off when Dick walked us through the 10 step Value Innovation Process. As a Strategy Consultant, working with executives to create models focused on growth through innovation and technology, I can say unequivocally that Dick Lee's Value Innovation Process has been transformational having the biggest impact on how we help our clients achieve their stated goals and objectives.

Alvin R. McBorrough
Managing Partner, Omnigroup, Centennial, CO
USA

"I have great pleasure in recommending "Value Innovation Works" to students and practitioners of Value Innovation. I have been reviewing the book chapter by chapter since the first draft was put out by Dr. Richard Lee. This is a timely effort in demystifying "Value Innovation". I believe "Value Innovation" is the core process that needs to be mastered if your goal is to grow your venture in to something really big. Since the economic meltdown of 2008 across global economies, there are many ups and downs across all asset classes, be it commodities, stocks, bonds or real estate. The volatile nature of these markets have put a brake on new investments and job creation. Existing businesses have also become very cautious and "risk averse".

Under these circumstances one would imagine new product and service introduction will seldom happen. However Value Innovators like Apple, Facebook, Google, Samsung and Jaguar/Land Rover keep introducing new products and services which are taking the market by storm. Their growth and valuation are apparently magical. How do they achieve this impossible feat?

While we do not know the exact processes followed by these value innovators, one conclusion that stares us in the face is that these companies are swimming in "Blue Oceans". Dr. Lee promises that following the methodology and tools given in the book one would certainly find a "Blue Ocean if it exists" in the market. While following any process it should be remembered that outcome of the process is always governed by robustness of the process and an element of chance. Sometimes the element of chance may favor the practitioner and it may result in a huge success; sometimes the element of chance may not favor the practitioner in which case the result may be muted. Process discipline guards the practitioner from huge downside even when chance does not favor. Dr. Lee presents a number of case studies which illustrate the abovc and make it amply clear that "Value Innovation Works".It is a robust,rigorous and repeatable process.

I've known Dr. Lee in a professional capacity for well over three years and I have used his methodology in my assignments a number of times. I have been impressed by the results.. I wish a great success for "Value Innovation Works".

R. Venkat Raman, Chief Strategist, Growth Navigators
Kolkata, India

"As an intellectual property consultant and business angel I firmly believe in innovation. However, my 'faith' had not yet found a 'religion' that amplified this 'faith' until I attended a workshop lead by Dick Lee. That day the business angel in me told me that I had to 'back this truck up'. The score of CEO's and R&D or marketing managers that also attended that workshop were all too deeply astonished by how quickly and easily we developed valuable insights with regard to defining the Most Important Customer in our Value Chains or the 'As Is' Value Curve. This really was some very feasible "Do It Yourself" stuff. I was in, I had found my 'religion'. I definitely wanted to become a member of this Value Innovation Tribe.

Dick Lee is a successful 'heretic' (marketing guru Seth Godin, "Tribes, We Need You to Lead Us", p. 70). As 'Lead Users' and believers in innovation, Dick and his colleagues created their own innovation 'religion' by challenging from within the variant that had won the most followers, namely Kim and Mauborgne's Value Innovation as described in their bible "Blue Ocean Strategy". Dick and Co. achieved this by mapping which elements of performance within Value Innovation mattered most to would-be innovators and to what extent. Then they had them vetted by their Most Important Customers. The end result is a business tool for the twenty first century.

The Value Innovation Process is not at all a 'command and obey tool' of a traditional factory, because it is a tool that enables: Bosses can lead by actively promoting the case for applying the Value Innovation Process to any aspect within the company, even with regard to their internal support functions. All they have to do is to find within the company their first 'partisans' and 'transform their shared interest in innovation into a passionate goal and desire for a change in innovation and to provide them with tools that allow the members to connect with themselves and set up the entire process'. For the rest the boss has to back off whenever possible (Tribes p. 21 & 50) and let that small tribe gradually change the entire corporate culture. (Hint: focus on the 'Top 5' characteristics out of a list of 25 in Chapter 1). In the end, everyone will be focused on the Most Important Customers within their Value Chains and they will be damn proud of it.

A Blue Ocean might still turn red some day, although the Value Innovation Process can help to delay sharks coming in by generating (1) intellectual property far more worth protecting and (2) a much better understanding as to what really deserves to be protected and as to how your innovation should be marketed. Moreover, the Value Innovation Process makes it very likely that ever more Blue Oceans will be created and that the best Value Innovators will do that regularly. That will be finally the time that equity analysts will feel compelled to review their already outdated views on innovation. Equity analysts don't lead, they follow.

Become a 'partisan' of the Value Innovation Tribe now and the rest will be history."

Pierre Saelen, business angel and intellectual property consultant
Owner of IP-Angels
Managing Director, Pharma Diagnostics
Brugge, Belgium

"This book outlines very explicitly the various aspects of applying the customer-in approach to new product or service introduction. The approach is a simple and very practical method to search and find innovation ideas based on the principals of Blue Ocean Strategy. The tools help to create development ideas for new or improved offerings related to the most important needs of your customers. So called commodities can be turned into attractive businesses!"

Frans van Giel, Corporate Vice President Group Business Development,
Sekhar Nettem, Group Business Development,
Formerly with NV Bekaert sa
Kortrijk, Belgium

"A must read if you want to implement a repeatable process consisting of a practical set of tools and techniques to help you discover what your most important customers really want and need!"

Johann Venter, Vice President Director R&D, AmVac
Newport Beach, CA,
USA

"In my career at a large energy company, I led or had key roles on over a hundred projects and during that time used many innovation methods, often within a project stage gate structure. In 2006, I led an effort to try out the Value Innovation Process on a project with internal customers and not only were opportunities to create exceptional value identified, but the contextual interviewing conversations created a strong "pull" from the internal customers to implement "their" opportunities. Following that successful project, I used the Value Innovation Process on dozens of projects, mostly with similar results. This book takes the reader on a journey illustrated with many industry examples to show how Value Innovation Works! I heartily recommend this book and innovation method for the true innovation practitioners".

Jim Weller, Co-Chair of the Mastering Value Innovation Best Practices Group.
Bay Area, CA, USA

"In this competitive market, every business would love to participate in a Blue Ocean. Value Innovation provides a comprehensive 10 step process that allows you to identify, develop, implement, and sustain a Blue Ocean opportunity. I participated in the first of several 2-Day Mastering Value Innovation Workshops held at our offices and came away having experienced the best training session in my 35 year career. With a third of our 350 employees being trained by Dick (Richard K. Lee) so far, we are committed to Value Innovation as an important mechanism to drive our growth. This training across all departments has helped us to build cross functional teams that now

have the tools and discipline required to enable American Vanguard to succeed."

Eric Wintemute, Chairman and CEO, American Vanguard Chemicals Corporation
Newport Beach, CA
USA

"The Value Innovation Process is fantastic! It brings innovation theory down to the working level with a well-defined process that yields tangible results.

The Value Innovation Process is changing the mindset within our company. It is just the reminder that we needed that our focus must continue to be delivering value to our customers.

We are using the Value Innovation Process to address some of our most challenging business issues. It is amazing how widely the VI approach can be applied. It has certainly changed the way we go about doing business! It has helped us realize that our business decisions need to take into account the customer's perspective as a foremost consideration."

Ed Wolf, Value Innovation Process Manager, Caterpillar Trimble Control Technologies.
Dayton, OH
USA

FOREWORD

The setting was a large conference room at a Denver airport hotel. The attendees were a battle-hardened mix of senior product managers and engineers, along with a healthy smattering of directors, VPs and C-Level executives who had flown in from all over the globe for the two-day workshop. The range of industries was as broad as the NASDAQ, DOW & S&P500 combined. The workshop was entitled "Mastering Value Innovation" and though I knew beforehand the general concepts that would be presented, nothing would prepare me for what was to happen over the two day workshop.

I (like most of you reading this foreword) have a deep interest and background in innovation, new product development and competitive strategy. Like most of you, I have read Blue Ocean Strategy, and have eagerly devoured most anything written by the innovation pantheon of Kim, Mauborgne, and Christensen. Like most of you, I have either led or been part of significant innovation initiatives in various companies, been to TED or watched TED talks, read Wired, Fast Company, HBR and follow 10-20 blogs daily, and yet in spite of all the reading, the planning, re-organizations etc., I have found myself flummoxed as to how to actually (and consistently) create innovative new products that customers delight in.

Denver changed everything. As we were learning the techniques that make up the Value Innovation Process (such as how to identify your most valuable customer, how to create an effective value curve, or how to do effective contextual interviewing) we were broken up into small groups of about 4-5 people. Each small group was asked to take the same medical product, and by applying the techniques we were learning, transform the product from a commodity to a breakthrough without sharing our work with the other groups. I watched as the 30 or so participants (myself included) in just a few short hours, took a product in a domain that none of us had expertise in (a specific nursing procedure), and created nearly identical solutions that very closely match the real world product breakthrough that a company experienced when applying these principles.

The lesson was clear - break through innovation can be taught, a series of steps can be followed, and a repeatable process can be put in place in any industry. More importantly, the techniques work without having to have the "creative genius" or the "rock star innovator" on the team. We didn't need to create a spinoff company to disrupt the parent company, we didn't need to hire expert consultants and we didn't even need to set up a separate R&D group (though there is nothing wrong with any of these things). What we needed to do was listen to the customer, understand their pain points, and through a well-defined collaborative process, provide a simple solution that would make their life better. What I learned in Denver you can learn and apply by reading this book.

As the world grows flatter it also grows faster. Crowdsourcing has created a participation economy that is unparalleled in history. While it took AOL 9 years to reach a million customers, it took Facebook 9 months, and the game Draw Something 9 days. Whether there is sustainable value in Draw Something (or even Facebook for that matter) over the long haul is perhaps questionable, but in the short term it highlights the challenging business environment that we find ourselves in.

A flatter, more connected world likely means that while your potential addressable market size grows, your revenues don't. We are facing the commoditization of nearly everything, and with technologies such as 3d printing becoming the newest rage, we could within the next few years easily see an economy where someone designs a simple product in the morning, and its available via 3d printing kiosks around the globe later that same day. Technological advances that had been reserved to some degree to the digital realm are becoming increasingly part of our physical world.

Deeply interconnected economies and an ever accelerating pace of business likely means more economic bubbles on the near horizon albeit with shorter life-spans yet with similar abilities to disrupt well crafted strategies and long term plans.

Customer's expectations continue to rise, as more and more niche companies are able to provide an ever-growing sea of products tightly tailored to small, custom markets quickly. Many of these smaller providers will go out of business in short order, disrupted by the very same principles they used to create their own market. But in a global economy there will be another start-up right behind them, ready to take their place.

The very principles of business, economics, money and value that have governed the developed world (and developing world to a lesser extent) for millennia, now seem to be shaken to the core. Many companies and many executives are at a loss as to how to proceed.

Some decide to focus on building-in more agility to their processes so they can produce products faster. This is certainly a core competency needed to remain competitive in the new world of business. But simply producing widgets faster (and or cheaper) is likely not going to be a sole sustaining strategy. No amount of Kaizen or army of six-sigma black belts will guarantee the sustainability or long term viability of your company.

Others, in the face of uncertainty, are spending more and more money on their social media strategies and are hiring bloggers, SEO experts, and twitter gurus to flood the digital space with their branding and ad campaigns, hoping that their legions of followers and "likes" will keep them afloat. Others are pouring significant dollars into mobile initiatives or pumping up their technology spending to try and gain a competitive edge via cool apps and integrated access to products and services.

Many are scaling up their R&D groups, hoping to find the killer product, while others are scaling back their spending on R&D to focus on "core competencies". Many are frustrated that their investments in R&D, or strategy and innovation initiatives seem to be yielding poor results. Chaos, confusion and even desperation reign supreme in many a manager's office and in many a boardroom around the globe.

Yet even if we can't predict the future, and may not have keen insight into our competitor's new "killer strategy" or where the markets will go next month, we can still future-proof our businesses and our economy and have a proven path forward for success. If you take a bigger picture historical view than simply the last few years, what comes clearly to light, even in times of great economic and/or political upheaval, is that customers will seek out and pay for real value, and societies that can provide that value will grow and thrive. This holds true around the world, across cultures, in times of peace, in times of war, in ages past and in our own present day.

Instead of trying to convert consumers to customers through sticky web or mobile portals, or try to increase customer loyalty through a rewards program, most companies would be better served in following the principles of Value Innovation which focus on delivering real value to your most important customer every time. Once these principles are in place, and become part of your company's DNA, all your other efforts will have a higher rate of return because they will be continually focused on real, sustainable value.

What Dr. Richard ("Dick") K. Lee, Nina Goodrich and their team have done is take the mystery out of innovation and apply a level of rigor to the science such that anyone who wants to can apply these principles and find success. These principles are not bound by industry vertical or product type, nor dependent on creative genius. Reflective of Dr. Lee's background not only in the hard sciences but his extensive worldwide business acumen – the processes and tools are universal and repeatable. Here finally is the "how" to go along with the "what" of innovation so that we can all start adding real value to our companies, our customers, our economy and even our nation. This is a timely book, and will add tools to your belt and strategies to your war chest that will serve you well in the midst of perhaps the most challenging business climate since the Renaissance.

Peter Frey
Vice President Digital Strategy and Delivery
Pearson
April 15, 2012
San Antonio, TX
United States of America

INTRODUCTION

This is a "How To Do It" book written by business people who have sat in your chair. I have worked with Nina Goodrich developing Value Innovation Tools and Methodology since 1999. Our Goal is to deliver the definitive book on innovation by walking you through the Value Innovation Process™ from start to finish using a down to earth, pragmatic approach.

Defining how to Deliver Exceptional Value to the Most Important Customer(s) in Your Value Chain, all the time, every time, you will find your Blue Oceans. And these Blue Oceans exist in markets you serve today. You will move mountains and drive sustainable, profitable growth. Throughout the book we provide many case studies and examples of companies and challenges. As you can see from the list below, we cover the landscape.

Value Innovation Process is a Trademark of Value Innovations, Inc.

ADM	B2B	Hussmann – Refrigerated cases	B2B
Alcan Pharmaceutical Packaging	B2B	International Airports – Their impact on the International Traveler	B2C
American Vanguard	B2B	Kodak	B2B & B2C
Ampex	B2B (B2C)	Knee Replacements for osteoarthritis patients in India – Johnson and Johnson, Smith and Nephew, and Stryker	B2C
Apple	B2C	Nokia	B2B & B2C
Carbon Motors E-7 Police Car	B2G	Procter and Gamble	B2B & B2C
Cargill	B2B	Replacement Auto Parts	B2B
Drywall manufacturers – Domtar, National & USG	B2B	RE/MAX International – Commercial and Residential real estate	B2B & B2C
Fibers used in Vehicle Armament Systems	B2B	Samsung Electronics – LCD TVs	B2C
FoldedPak – ExpandOS packaging material	B2B & B2C	Sharp	B2C
Ford Interceptor Police Car	B2G	Sony	B2C
GlaxoSmithKline – Sensodyne Repair and Protect Toothpaste with Novamin	B2C	Virgin Mobile "Pay as You Go" cell phone service	B2C

Enabling tools are explained in detail and examples provided. At the end of each chapter you will find Next Steps and Takeaways sections. Any organization of any size, for profit or not-for-profit, manufacturing or services based company, a federal, state or local government agency, an association or charitable organization, a university, school or school board, can benefit from Value Innovation Works. As long you have a customer you can use the Value Innovation Process and tools. If you work in a support function, e.g., IT, HR, finance, and purchasing, your Most Important Customer is inside your organization. Are you Delivering Exceptional Value to them?

The target audiences are: equity investors, venture capitalists and angel investors; deans and professors at universities and business schools; university students; officials at the Federal, State and local government levels; school board members and school districts; staffs of not-for-profit organizations and associations; and CEO's, COO's, VPs, directors, managers and project leaders of publicly traded and privately held companies.

We started the Review Process mid February, 2012. Over the ensuing 6 weeks, we worked with 19 Reviewers in Belgium, Brazil, England, Germany, India, Italy, and the US. They devoted their valuable time critiquing each chapter and sharing their thoughts to help us improve the book. We received more than 100 Chapter Reviews. We provided Reviewers with four or five statements to rate each Chapter. Using a 1 to 7 scale (1 – I very Strongly Disagree and 7 – I Very Strongly Agree) the average rating for all reviews was 5.7. We are overwhelmed!

I thank our reviewers for their tremendous support, the time they invested and their efforts which substantially improved the value of every Chapter. They are our heroes!

This first group reviewed up to five chapters:

Ricardo de Carvalho - Geroma do Brasil, Brazil	Larry McKeogh - Broad Leaf Product Design, USA
Stefania Fraccon - Whirlpool, Italy	Ludita Vallarta – IRI, USA
Erick Gamas – UOP, USA	Jeff Wallace - University of Illinois at Urbana-Champaign, USA
Paul Germeraad - Intellectual Assets, Inc., USA	Jim Weller – Co-Chair of the Mastering Value Innovation Best Practices Group, USA
Markus Heinen - Ernst and Young, Germany	Ed Wolf - Caterpillar Trimble Control Technologies, USA
Steve Hinton - Hinton Sheerline Ltd., England	

The second group of Reviewers read every chapter....over the top dedication to the task at hand!

Joan Garland - Friend and avid reader of nonfiction books, USA	Pent Penton - President, Innovation Insights, USA
Andrew Gelfand – Sales Manager, Achiewell LLC, USA	Venkat Raman - Chief Strategist, Growth Navigators, India
Bruce Janda – Group Innovation Leader, AstenJohnson, USA	Terry Say – Principal, Say Consulting LLC, USA
Fernando Machado - CEO, Focototal, Ltd., Brazil	

...and then there's Pierre Saelen – Business Angel, IP angels and Managing Director, Pharma Diagnostics, Belgium. Pierre dissected chapters using his lawyer's microscope, put his analysis in the top drawer, reconsidered the following morning, and sent his final thoughts on to me. It was Pierre who suggested we put together a set of icons circling the Most Important Customer and put it on the front cover. Why? To underscore the Most Important Customer and the Value Innovation Process are at the heart of Value Innovation Works. Pierre, Thank You!

What was the impetus for finally writing this book? Lin, my wife, and I were having dinner with forty attendees of Pure-Insights' Value Innovation Masterclass, just outside Schiphol Airport in Amsterdam. It was January 18, 2012, and the weather was truly mid-January, but the group was very excited and really fired up. Upmost on their minds? They wanted to know why we hadn't written the definitive book. The message... "You have to do this!" We started writing in early February and, three months later, we published the book.

... and enabling this?

- Createspace.com. They are Value Innovators in the book publishing space!
- Kathy Reed, DesignByKreation in NE England, who took the pain out of publishing online. Kathy, thank you for a job very well done!

Lin has been my Muse. She edited and, as usual, cleaned up my excess verbiage. We work extremely well together, focusing on common goals: Deliver exceptional value to You; Complete the book in 3 months. And, we made it. Every Chapter was exciting! The value delivered to you, the reader, Our Most Important Customer, is ultimately, our responsibility. If you enjoy it, please recommend it to your peers and network!
I have many things to thank Lin for in my life and this is very high on that list!

Richard ("Dick") K. Lee
CEO and Chief Innovation Officer – Value Innovations, Inc.,
Castle Pines Village, CO
United States of America
May 1, 2012

CONTENTS

CHAPTER 1

"Innovation is the specific tool of entrepreneurs, the means by which they exploit change as an opportunity for a different business or a different service. It is capable of being presented as a discipline, capable of being learned, capable of being practiced. Entrepreneurs need to search purposefully for the sources of innovation, the changes and their symptoms that indicate opportunities for successful innovation. And they need to know and to apply the principles of successful innovation."

Peter F. Drucker

Why do we innovate? What is innovation?

How do we innovate?

The ability to innovate determines the growth, sustainability and agility of companies and countries. Whether you are the President of the USA, the owner of a restaurant in Liverpool, a farmer in Queensland, the Governor of Colorado, a taxi driver in Singapore, or the CEO of a publicly traded company, you share the common belief that a country's economy must grow. With healthy GDP growth, people are happy because their standard of living is improving. The engine for this growth is innovation.

While there are as many interpretations of innovation as there are grains of sand, we define Value Innovation as "Delivering exceptional value to the Most Important Customer in the Value Chain, all the time, every time." Whether your organization is a not-for-profit, B2B, B2C, B2G, a government agency, large, small or in between, whether your Most Important Customer is outside or inside the organization, you can value innovate. If you have a customer, the Value Innovation Process will work for you.

As you read Value Innovation Works, you will experience working examples of contemporary companies who used Value Innovation methodologies and tools with great success. Ask Brad Fehn how the Process and Tools worked at FoldedPak. FoldedPak's product, ExpandOS, is an environmentally acceptable replacement for bubble-wrap, peanuts and foam packing materials. The VCs, investing $7 million in FoldedPak from 2004 to 2009, faced the decision to either completely change direction or close the doors. ExpandOS was a great idea going nowhere. The VCs brought Brad in to see what could be done to save the company. Using the Value Innovation Process™, FoldedPak focused on their Most Important Customers in both the B2B and B2C spaces. The company was quickly turned around and ExpandOS is a huge success today. FoldedPak's customers include: Canada Post, CoorsTek, hp, Home Depot, National Semi Conductor, Paragon Pumps and Staples.

Value Innovation Works describes a 10-Step Value Innovation Process and a set of enabling tools that are strong levers of change. Implementing the Value Innovation Process makes company associates think and behave differently!

The Value Innovation Process will uncover "What" and "How" you will Deliver Exceptional Value to the Most Important Customer in your Value Chains. You will understand when a company Value Innovates consistently, it drives sustainable,

Value Innovation Process is a Trademark of Value Innovations, Inc.

profitable growth. It follows when many companies Value Innovate, their country will experience healthy economic growth.

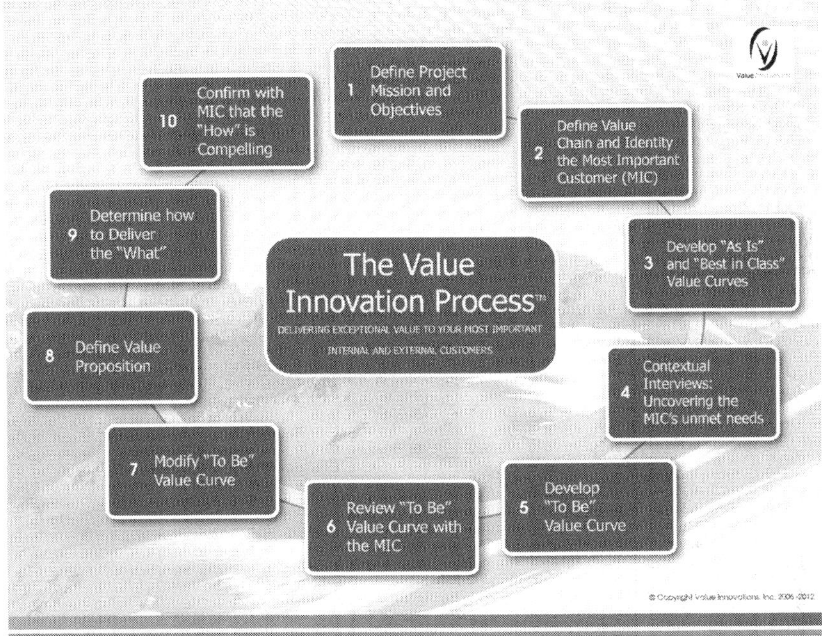

To assure success, a company needs a commitment from all parties involved. When the CEO/president/managing director of your company is on board and all members of the leadership team are committed, your company will become a Value Innovator.

The Value Innovation Process bolts onto the front end of your company's Stage-Gate, Phase-Gate or Toll Gate Process. It is the Front End of Innovation. We recommend you review your existing new product and service development processes and determine how to best combine the Value Innovation Process. You may find the need to reduce the number of steps or change the order of steps. If it accomplishes the desired result, make the changes.

When the focus is on the Most Important Customer outside the organization, the Value Innovation Process can be used to develop new strategies, new business models, new products, new services, new delivery methods, new packaging, technology roadmaps, etc.

When the focus is on the Most Important Customer inside the organization, support functions can use the Value Innovation Process to address a multitude of unmet needs:

e.g., 1. Human Resources: Develop a Performance Appraisal Process that is more user friendly, decreases the calendar processing time by at least 50%, reduces the paperwork by at least 50%, and makes outcomes much clearer to the individual being appraised.

e.g., 2. Purchasing: Develop a new system that allows individuals to order product from an approved catalog of products and services that uses the same framework for all the BUs and is as easy to use as ordering a book from Amazon, allowing them to bypass purchasing.

e.g., 3. IT: Develop apps and software for the iPad3 so their sales people can provide instant answers to their customer's questions when they are on a sales call.

The process can also be used to address manufacturing problems.

Each of the 10 Steps in the Value Innovation Process is

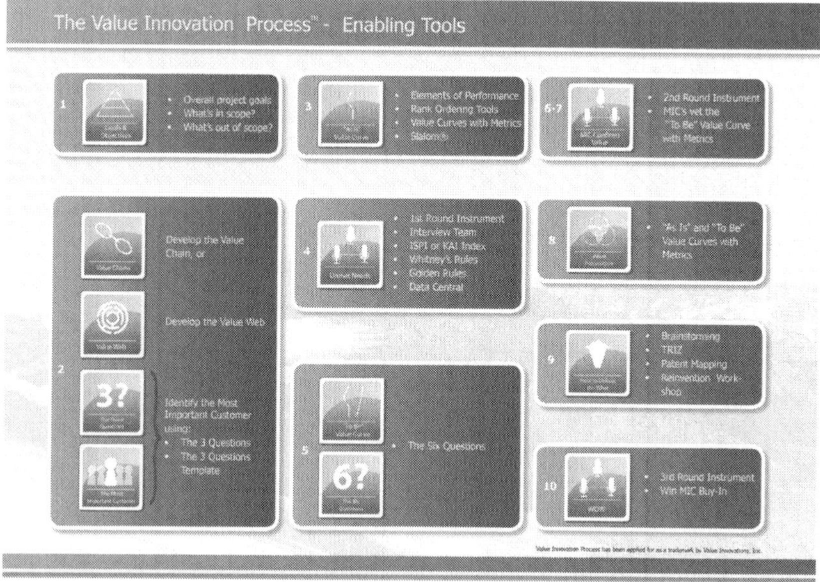

executed using a rigorous approach, facilitated by a set of enabling tools. Typically the Value Innovation Process takes 10 to 12 weeks to complete. The primary tools are shown in the previous figure.

In an effort to concisely clarify the characteristics of an innovative company, the following table defines high and low level of maturity in innovation. This is based on our collective business experiences (over 70 years). Are there innovative companies operating at a high level in all these characteristics? No, not even Apple, with their sales increasing by $48B from 2010 to 2011. If you have checked off a majority of low levels of innovation maturity, you have work to do!

	Characteristics of a Company with a High Level of Innovation Maturity	Characteristics of a Company with a Low Level of Innovation Maturity
A	Leadership and Strategy	
1	CEO champions innovation (this could also be the Managing Director or Business Unit head).	Innovation is probably being led by a group in R&D or marketing.
2	Company strategy is clearly defined and understood by all employees. The link between strategy and innovation strategy is clear.	Strategy is developed by the senior leadership team, has the detail of an operating plan, fills a 3" ring binder and picks up dust when it's finished. There is no innovation strategy.
3	Company balances meeting quarterly and current year results with the requirement to invest in the future to support sustainable long term growth.	Company focused primarily on next quarter's results.

B	Customer Focus	
1	See their customers as their most important stakeholder.	See shareholders as their most important stakeholder.
2	Focus is on delivering value to customers.	Focus is on delivering value to the company. EPS, ROI and NPV are of paramount importance.
3	Company has rigorous processes in place to uncover customers' unmet needs. All employees have access to the insights.	Sales "owns" the customer, and few people outside of Sales are allowed access to customers.
C	Innovation	
1	Company has at least one corporate goal that drives innovation.	No goals driving innovation.
2	There is an innovation process and it's used on all projects.	No innovation process.
3	Innovation is clearly defined and understood throughout the organization.	Innovation is a buzzword and probably used a lot too.
4	Executive compensation tied to innovation goals.	Executive compensation not tied to innovation.
5	Innovation goals are in place down to the mid manager level.	Line managers aren't held accountable for mentoring new business initiatives and lack specific innovation goals.
6	Metrics to track innovation (# of projects, inputs, outputs, success rates, contribution to sales and profit growth) are in	There are no metrics to track innovation.

	place, reported, rewarded and celebrated.	
D	Management and Training	
1	Project leaders bust through walls. They are the company's future GMs.	Project leaders are average performers and have no career path.
2	A significant percentage of employees have been trained in innovation and enabling tools. An innovation training curriculum is in place and is updated regularly.	Few, if any, employees have been trained as innovators.
3	Manage Risk: Taking appropriate risk is encouraged and rewarded	Risk averse.
4	Low # of projects/FTE. Ideally 1: Use collocated, dedicated project teams.	High # of projects/FTE. Engineers and R&D people assigned to too many projects and do a poor job on most of them.
E	Culture and Environment	
1	See employees/associates as value creators.	See employees as a cost and dispensable.
2	People are empowered: Project leaders have authority that matches the responsibility.	Project leaders have responsibility but no authority.
3	Excellent communications.	Tough to find out what's going on.
4	It's exciting and fun to work in this company.	Work is a grind here.
5	Functional areas collaborate.	Functional areas are

		siloed.
6	Proactive: Important beats out the urgent most of the time.	Reactive: Urgent trumps the important every time (you'll see people at meetings, phone in one hand texting and a laptop checking email).
7	Support functions looking to provide value to the BUs they serve.	Support functions make work for the BUs.
F	**Decision Making and Cycle Times**	
1	Make decisions quickly... delegated down.	Decisions take a long time... relegated up.
2	Cycle times are being reduced.	Lean and 6 sigma are on a roll.

Sources of these characteristics: The Value IQ Tool (1); The Value Innovation Process Assessment Tool (2); Identify your innovation enablers and inhibitors (3); Hamel's 10 Rules for Bubbling Up Billion dollar ideas (4); Gary Hamel, "What Happens Now." (5)

These two levels of innovation maturity highlight major differences in focus and behavior. To transition from a low level to a high level of maturity takes a significant effort and it does not happen overnight. As an example, A G Lafley spent his nine years as CEO of P&G driving to a higher level of innovation maturity (6).

Should we assume that all companies are transitioning from a Lower Level to a Higher Level of Maturity? No, there are examples where the reverse is true, e.g., Kodak. The following quotes excerpted from "Kodak in Crisis - Snapshot of a humbled giant" (7), speak to the danger of focusing on quarterly results and bowing to analysts. Referring to the table above, Kodak was moving away from:

- "Balances meeting quarterly and current year results with the requirement to invest in the future to support sustainable long term growth"
- "Seeing their customers as their most important stakeholder"
- "Focus is on delivering value to customers"

Kodak moved towards:

- "Focusing primarily on next quarter's results"
- "Seeing shareholders as their most important stakeholder"
- "Focusing on delivering value to the company."
- "EPS, ROI and NPV are of paramount importance."

"Mary Benner, associate professor at the University of Minnesota's Carlson School of Management, has studied equity analysts' reactions to the strategies of companies facing radical technological change in the newspaper, telecoms and photographic sectors. She concluded they were "more attentive and positive" towards those companies that tried to extend and preserve the old technology. One analyst in 1994 referred to Kodak "squandering" investors' money on "digital nonsense" (8).

Even in 1999, when analysts were more positive about digital strategies, they still warned about the potential cannibalization of the film business. "[Kodak] was stuck on film and Wall Street was doing nothing to discourage it," says Prof Benner. Far from being the "moving target" George Eastman had hoped to create, Kodak was in danger of becoming a sitting duck."

Forced to select a "Top 5" innovation characteristics list to focus on from our list of 25, we select:

- The CEO champions innovation (Leadership)
- The company sees its customers as its most important stakeholder (Customer Focus)

- The company has at least one corporate goal that drives innovation (Innovation)
- The company is proactively using the Value Innovation Process on all major initiatives (Innovation)
- Project leaders bust through walls. They are the company's future GMs (Management and Training)

With these five in place and working well, we have seen company culture, company environment and stakeholder behavior change for the better. To illustrate this phenomenon we have included three examples:

- A paper products company: Sales reps were reluctant to have a team contextually interviewing their customers – "I talk to my customers, nobody else can because they will just louse up the account." The team negotiated a deal with the sales reps where the sales reps could be with their customer(s) during the interview. The sales reps agreed not to ask questions or interfere with the process but they could take the customer out to lunch or dinner afterwards. Seeing the process in action and the very positive feedback from the customer, the sales reps were sold on the process and became enablers.
- A publicly traded specialty chemical company: The CEO and CTO are both champions. This feedback came from one of their Product Managers seven months after Value Innovation training started: "I spent the last week at our headquarters for a managers' meeting for all departments in our company. Value Innovation was brought up in several presentations. Our CTO has integrated Value Innovation into our organization successfully. It is working wonders for our general processes, thought process, and marketing department."
- A joint venture between two publicly traded companies: The Business Unit head is the champion. Project teams were having difficulty recruiting Most Important Customers because their dealers were not supporting the process. They either did not provide customer names and

contact information and/or did not share how the interviews would be carried out and did not endorse the process. One project team was successful in recruiting twelve Most Important Customers. The results from this project were shared at a meeting with many dealers. It was the highlight of the 2-Day event. The dealers were so impressed with the results, they transformed from being inhibitors to enablers.

Success breeds success and slowly but surely, you will see "Not Invented Here" and the Corporate Immune System are pushed back. The old rule applies, "Start small but think Big." The Value Innovation Process does work.

A commitment to innovation requires not only a change in culture and behavior but attention to the basics as well. Innovation must be defined, understood and used the same way by everyone in the organization. It must become the company's core, the veritable fabric of its existence. Left open to interpretation, the process becomes unfocused, the results, disappointing and in the extreme cases, the company disappears.

As we have mentioned, there are numerous definitions of innovation. In an effort to clarify the different theories of Innovation, we have developed the following Table of 14 different forms of innovation in use today (Table 1). For an explanation of these terms, refer to the Glossary of Terms:

Table 1: Fourteen Forms of Innovation in Use Today

	Form of Innovation	Proponent/Guru
1	Classical Innovation	John Bessant (University of Exeter) and Joe Tidd (University of Sussex) – UK (9,10)
2	Customer Centric Innovation	Eric von Hippel (MIT) – USA (11-13)
3	Disruptive Innovation	Clayton Christensen (Harvard) – USA (14-16)
4	Management Innovation	Gary Hamel (The Management Lab) – USA (4,5, 17)Ricardo Semler (Semco) – Brazil (18,19)
5	Open Innovation	Henry Chesbrough (UC Berkeley) – USA (20,21)
6	Orbit Shifting Innovation	Rajiv Narang and P Munshi (Erewhon) and Bhupendra Sharma (NXTLYF) – India (22)
7	Outcome Driven Innovation	Tony Ulwick (Strategyn) – USA(23)
8	Radical Innovation	Mark Rice (Bentley) and Gina O'Connor (RPI) – USA (24)
9	Relentless Innovation	Jeffrey Phillips (OVO/NetCentrics) – USA (25)
10	Reverse Innovation	Vijay Govindarajan and Chris Trimble (Dartmouth) – USA (26)
11	Stage-Gate Innovation	Bob Cooper and Scott Edgett (Product Development Institute) – Canada (27)
12	Strategic Innovation	Constantinos Markides (London Business School) – UK(28)
13	Value Innovation	W Chan Kim, Renée Mauborgne (INSEAD) – France (29, 30) Richard K. Lee (Value Innovations, Inc.) – USA (1)
14	4th Generation R&D (Innovation)	Bill Miller (4G Innovation LLC), Langdon Morris – USA (31)

While the gurus, most of whom are academics, have made significant contributions, those of us in industry are still left with burning questions. Unlike all the others cited in Table 1 we did not invent a new category of innovation, however we innovated in the Value Innovation space. What matters in Value Innovation is: "Where do I start? How do I start? What do I do? What do I do next? Can I afford the effort? "Is it also applicable to my unit/team?" Value Innovations Works starts where the gurus stop. We describe a Process that works by putting Your Most Important Customers at the center of your universe. We do not use big words, just facts, processes and results. Readers who previously used other innovation advice, can rest assured, the interesting parts can be incorporated into the Value Innovation Process or can follow on where it stops, i.e., bolt onto the front end of your stage- gate process (27).

We trace the beginnings of the current thinking on Value Innovation to C. K. Prahalad (32,33), Dean of the Ross Business School at the University of Michigan. Susan Berfield (34) wrote in Bloomberg BusinessWeek, April 22, 2010, "C. K. Prahalad, who died April 16, at 68, was hell-bent on shaking managers free of what he called "Dominant Logic", deeply held assumptions about the world. He was a pro-active thinker who regularly came up with startling insights that would send executives scrambling. As a teacher, C. K. nudged his students to stretch their minds. As a consultant, he demanded his clients do the same." Three of his graduate students, Constantinos Markides, Gary Hamel and W. Chan Kim, built upon C. K.'s work, developed their own theories and advanced Innovation thinking as a result.

Constantinos Markides (Strategic Innovation), Professor of Strategic Leadership at the London Business School, published All the Right Moves, November, 1999 (28). A highly practical handbook on the fundamentals of strategy, it helps managers zero in on the critical choices that lie at the heart of all innovative strategies. He argues that even the best strategies have a limited life leading companies to continually create and implement new strategic positions. This leads to innovation by breaking the rules of the game. This is accomplished with creative thinking that leads to strategic innovation - the "breakthroughs" that separate winning strategies from those that can be called also-rans. In this theory, strategic thinking is a creative process, not merely a data gathering process. Markides works at developing strategic thinking skills to make the tough choices that all business strategists must face to find the "breakthroughs".

Gary Hamel (Management Innovation), Director of The Management Lab and a good friend of Costas Markides, sets out the following hypothesis in both Strategy is Revolution (17) and Leading the Revolution (35). In every market, there are:

1. Rule Makers – They are number one in the markets they serve. (e.g., BASF, BMW (in luxury cars), ExxonMobil, P&G, Toyota, WalMart) and set the rules for the Rule Takers.
2. Rule Takers - They play by the rules set by the Rule Maker.
3. Rule Breakers – Set and play by their own rules with the goal of becoming the Rule Makers of the future (e.g., Apple (now a Rule Maker), Dyson, USA Today, Virgin Group).

Gary Hamel published "10 rules for bubbling up billion-dollar ideas" in Fortune in June, 2000 (4). They are:

1. Set unreasonable expectations (If the market you serve grows at 5% and your business plan calls for 5% growth, you have not set an unrealistic expectation)
2. Stretch your business definition (Be prepared to move into areas adjacent to your competencies)
3. Create a cause, not a business (Associates are highly motivated)
4. Listen to new voices (Move outside your traditional customer base)
5. Design an open market for ideas (Seek ideas from outside).

6. Offer an open market for capital (Be prepared to fund attractive new ideas when they appear).
7. Open up the market for talent (Put your best talent on your high priority projects to maximize the chances of success)
8. Lower the risks of experimentation.
9. Make like a cell: divide and divide (Keep business units small like Illinois Tool Works)
10. Pay your innovators really well.

Most recently, Gary Hamel published "What Matters Now." (5) He shares many insights. These captured our attention:

- We owe our future to innovation.
- Today, human beings confront a daunting array of problems that demand new solutions. Climate change, global pandemics, failed states, narco-crime, terrorism, nuclear proliferation, environmental degradation – meeting these challenges will require us to invent new innovation systems. We have to solve problems that are multidimensional and multijurisdictional.

W. Chan Kim and Renée Mauborgne (Value Innovation), Professors at INSEAD, introduced the term Value Innovation in their paper, Value Innovation: The Strategic Logic of High Growth, Jan/Feb, 1997 (29). In this paper they share how Accor used Value Innovation logic to reinvent Formule1, a French hotel chain. In March, 2005, Kim and Mauborgne published Blue Ocean Strategy (30). They postulated companies should render the competition irrelevant, i.e., moving away from red oceans of intense competition, and create "blue oceans" of uncontested market space. This creates powerful leaps in value for both the company and its customers. Blue Ocean Opportunities (uncontested market spaces) can exist in the markets you are serving today. When you use the Value Innovation Process, we do not guarantee you will find a Blue Ocean Opportunity, but we do guarantee, if a Blue Ocean Opportunity exists, you will surface it.

Based on Value Innovation logic, Blue Ocean Strategy has been translated into 42 languages and has sold over 2.8 Million copies. It has influenced the thinking of many CEOs around the world. Blue Ocean Strategy is the most successful book in the history of Harvard Business School Press. It is a theory. It describes the result. It does not define the process on how to render the competition irrelevant. Questions such as: Where do I start? How do I start? What do I do? What do I do next? are not answered.

The first attempt to define the Value Innovation Process (see diagram below) was published in "Value Innovation: Passport to Wealth Creation" in March, 2005 (1). It resulted from work carried out by representatives from >50 Industrial Research Institute (http://www.iriweb.org/) companies working on a Research on Research sub-committee (RoR 99-07: "Value Creation through Value Innovation") during the period 1999-2002. It was a good start but it was complicated and lacked a set of enabling tools.

The first Value Innovation Process

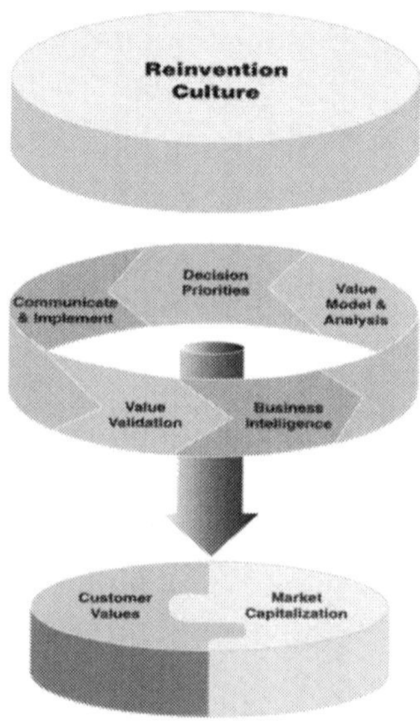

During the period 2002 - 2012, the 10-Step Value Innovation Process as we know it today took shape. It embraces the thinking of CK Prahalad, Henry Chesbrough, Clayton Christensen, Costas Markides, Gary Hamel, W Chan Kim/Renee Mauborgne, and others. More importantly, it has been used and tested in companies/organizations like yours.

Apple is the innovation exemplar. Steve Jobs was not our client, but what he did at Apple proves our point that innovation pays. On March 28, 1996, a headline in The New York Times declared, "On Monday, Moody's Investors Service Inc. said that it was downgrading Apple's $305 million of senior debt to junk bond status." When Jobs returned to Apple in August, 1997, the company was losing $1B a year, held just 4% of the PC market, and was losing market share. The stock was worth $5.45 split adjusted. Michael Dell, CEO of Dell computer, said at the time, "I'd shut Apple down and give the money back to the shareholders." (36) - Business Week. October 6, 1997.

In just 14 years, Apple is the most valuable company in the world and the world's largest technology company. Apple stock closed at $605.23 on April 13, 2012. That is an increase of > 7000%. Apple's net sales increased 66% from $65.2B in 2010 to $108.3B in 2011. Apple sold 37 million iPhones (up 128% from 2010), 15.4 million iPads (up 111% from 2010) and 5.2 million Macs (up 26% from 2010) in the 4th quarter of 2011. In 4Q, 2011 they became the world market share leaders in smart phones and tablets (37). Steve Jobs championed innovation and established an incredible legacy/stage for Apple to continue sustainable, profitable growth (38).

During this period 1997 to 2011, Apple did not invent anything! Not the MP3 player, not the mobile phone, not recording, not TV and not the tablet. What did Apple do? They innovated. They took existing technology and packaged it in products and services, meticulously attending to every detail inside and outside, down to the exquisite packaging. They delivered exceptional value to the consumer. They innovated; they did not invent. Jobs fondly remembered a quote from

Picasso, "Good artists copy, great artists steal", "and at Apple we have always been shameless about stealing great ideas."

As an example, we will review the innovation of the iPod. Sony owned the market with the Walkman. Cast your mind back to Gary Hamel's "10 Rules for bubbling up billion dollar ideas". There is no evidence to suggest that Steve Jobs consciously put these into use, but most of them are in evidence in Apple's success. Steve Jobs did, however, read and use the thoughts of Clayton Christiansen's Disruptive Innovation. Clayton Christiansen postulated, "Markets that do not exist, cannot be analyzed. Suppliers and customers must discover them together." Steve Jobs and his teams saw portable music as a market. They implemented the integration of hardware, software, devises and content sales. At Apple, Jobs was intimately involved. He pushed all of his teams to work as one cohesive and flexible team. The result was the iPod nano, iTunes Store, etc. A world we cannot live without. Sony could not compete. It was a siloed organization.

You do not have to be the Wright brothers inventing flight, Thomas Edison inventing the light bulb, Bell labs inventing the transistor or DARPA inventing the internet to supercharge your organization. Any company can Value Innovate and drive sustainable, profitable growth. This book shows you how.

Ampex: Invention without innovation does not insure success. There are many examples of "first ones in" failing. Ampex Invented a seminal technology: The ability to record audio and video on the same medium in the 1950s.

Ampex, Redwood City, CA (15 miles from Apple's headquarters). The Ampex name on Route 101 is all that is left of a once proud company.

The first delayed TV broadcast was successfully transmitted on November 30, 1956 with Ampex's VR-1000A.

Ampex's stock rocketed from 50¢ to $350. However, Ampex had a low level of innovation maturity and was not prepared to make the investments in tape drives, tapes, displays, and semiconductors, etc. to reduce the cost. Japanese consumer electronics companies licensed the technology from Ampex, made the required investments and introduced VCRs that were affordable in the consumer market. Ampex filed for Chapter 7 bankruptcy, and they closed the doors in March, 2008.

Are there other Ampex's? Blockbuster, Circuit City, Olivetti, Polaroid, and Xerox come to mind. Are there others following in their footsteps? Best Buy, Carrefour, Nokia, RIM and Sony appear to be going in the wrong direction.

We do not want this to happen to your company and we have pointed to many warning signs. Booz and Company, 2011 Global 1000 Innovation survey reported that only one half of the 1000 Companies think their culture robustly supports an innovation strategy or that their innovation strategy supports their corporate strategy. Value Innovation is a practical, repeatable process to drive sustainable, profitable growth.

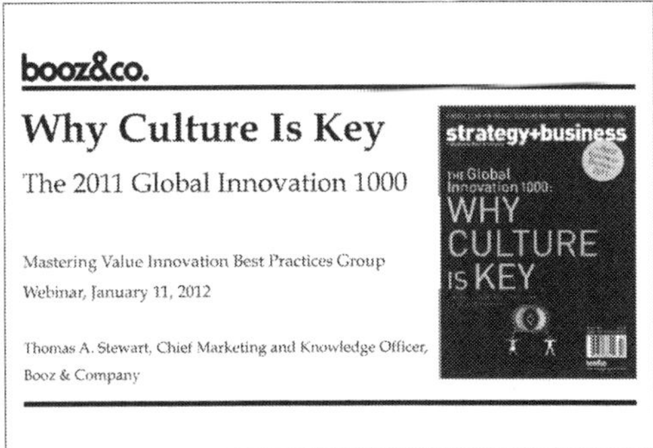

In this report, Booz and Company divided the 1000 companies into three categories: Need Seekers, Market Readers and Technology Drivers. As a group, these 1000 companies invested $550B, about 48% of the total global R&D spend in 2010. Need Seekers focused on addressing their customers' problems and unmet needs. They did not invent, they innovated. The Top 10 Need Seekers grew faster (28%) and were more profitable (41%) than the Top 10 R&D spenders. Fast Company also carried out an Innovation survey. Booz and Company's and Fast Company's "Top 10" Innovators in 2011 are compared in the Table 2 below:

Table 2: A comparison of Booz and Company's and Fast Company's "Top 10" Innovators in 2011

Rank	Booz and Company's "Top 10" Innovators in 2011	Fast Company's "Top 10" Innovators in 2011 (39)
1	Apple	Apple
2	Google	Twitter
3	3M	Facebook
4	GE	Nissan
5	Microsoft	Groupon
6	IBM	Google
7	Samsung	Dawning Information Industry
8	P&G	Netflix
9	Toyota	Zynga
10	Facebook	Epocrates

Booz and Company's list was selected from the list of the 1,000 largest R&D investors by CEO's. There are only three on the Booz and Company list that appear on Fast Company's list: Apple, Google and Facebook. Does this put to bed once and for all the argument that R&D investment is a measure of innovativeness? We hope so.

Strange though it may seem, we have seen many companies who develop new products and services without ever talking to a customer. They develop a solution first and then go out to the market to look for problems to solve. We call it "armchair marketing". It leads to inconsistent product launches, flowery value propositions, and a constant stream of mixed messages, product recalls and irritated customers. It is fueled by a corporate logic that seems too focused on "inventing our way to success in R&D labs".

Here is an elegant example of how to do it right. In 2005, Samsung Electronics decided to increase sales of LCD TVs by 1 million in the US market. They had less market share than Sony and competed on a par with Sharp. Samsung concluded they needed to reduce price and increase the value delivered on design after talking to the customer. As a result of understanding their customer's mindset and making the required changes, Samsung's share of the US LCD market rocketed from 12.1% in January, 2006 to 26.4% five months after introducing the Series 51/52 (Bordeaux) product line (40).

As you proceed through the 10 Step Value Innovation Process in the following Chapters, each Step is mapped out and fully explained using examples such as Samsung to illustrate the Step. This is a practical application that you can use to influence the shift in your organization to become a Value Innovation Organization.

Next Steps:

1. Send an email to your peers and ask them how they would define innovation. Collate the responses and share them with the group.
2. Use the 25 characteristics to determine level of innovation maturity in your company. Prepare a maturity level assessment, send it out, collate the date and share with your CEO.
3. Prepare for a journey/roadmap into the exciting world of Value Innovation.

Takeaways:

1. Take a page from Steve Jobs' playbook: The CEO/Managing Director/Business Unit head is the Value Innovation champion driving sustainable, profitable growth.

2. Your company needs a strategy and a definition of innovation that everyone in your company agrees to.
3. Your company needs at least one innovation goal.
4. Have a clear definition of, and support for, Value Innovation across your organization.
5. Train associates on how to Value Innovate.
6. Each function in your organization is responsible for Value Innovation. Be passionate about the business and have fun.
7. To keep focus and retain momentum, make decisions quickly and reduce cycle times.
8. Reduce individual workloads when you adopt, install and use the Value Innovation Process.

CHAPTER 2

"I believe that this nation should commit itself to achieving the goal, before this decade is out, of landing a man on the moon and returning him safely to the earth."

John F Kennedy, May 25, 1961

Value Innovation Process Step #1:

Define the Overall Project Goals and Objectives

In one sentence President Kennedy defined the targeted completion date and what needed to be accomplished for the "Man on the Moon" project. The first step in the Value Innovation Process is to clearly define the project objectives, key project details and the project scope.

This raises the question, "Who defines the new project, the overall goal and objectives?" The answer is simple. Anybody in the organization can make suggestions, ask questions. It could be the CEO, the head of manufacturing or the newest hire. If the company has a Value Innovation Process Manager, we recommend that these suggestions be directed to his/her office. The Value Innovation Process Manager should meet with the submitter and complete the following template. The Value Innovation Project Manager would share the output with the team responsible for reviewing, and prioritizing the front end of innovation projects. This team would make a "Go"/"No Go" decision on the proposed project:

- The CEO may ask, "What are our best options to double the size of our company in three years staying within the limits of our adjacent core competencies?"
- The head of manufacturing could ask, "Customers are asking us to deliver our products in a far more environmentally friendly way. What are our best options to do this?"
- The head of marketing may ask, "How could we change our business models to deliver much greater value to our Most Important Customers?"
- The new hire may suggest, "How are we providing, configuring and installing apps on Tablets for our sales force to answer our Most Important Customers questions in real time?"

We assume that all organizations have their own form of project management. Therefore we conclude little guidance is needed in this area. We suggest that if a project has been ongoing for a number of years, or the personnel on the project team have changed, or the project is unfocused at this time, the following template could be a helpful reset:

Project Name:
Project Champion:
Project Leader:
Overall Goal:
Objectives: 1. ______ 2. ______ 3. ______ 4. ______

Project Start Date:	Targeted Complete Date:
Expense Budget:	
Project Team Members:	
What's in Scope?:	What's out of Scope?:

It is critical to define "What is in scope" and "what is out of scope?" The following example illustrates the importance of clearly defining project scope.

American Vanguard, a $300MM publicly traded company headquartered in Newport Beach, CA, develops, markets and manufactures biocides, pesticides, fungicides and fertilizers. American Vanguard used Value Innovations' 10 Step Process in a project with the following objective: Deliver insecticide/nematocide to banana trees with no negative environmental impact in geographical areas draining to creeks and rivers using the current active ingredient in the insecticide.

A product was used to spray the root systems of banana trees in Costa Rica. It is 100% effective in killing nematodes which attack the banana tree roots that dramatically reduce fruit production by the tree. It was not suited for use near aquatic habitats,

Deliver insecticide/nematicide to banana trees with no negative environmental impact in areas close to creeks and rivers using the current active ingredient

What's in scope?

- New delivery method
- New Formulation

What's out of scope?

- New active ingredients

however new plantations had boundaries far away from streams and rivers to minimize fish kill from runoff when it rained. It rains a lot in Costa Rica.

The probability that AmVac could develop a new active ingredient (new molecule) as effective as the current molecule without adverse impact in streams and rivers was very low. Also, the development time would be long. A minimum of 10 years would be required to go through the regulatory approval process. The conclusion: a new active ingredient (new molecule) was deemed to be "Out Of Scope."

By making the New Active Ingredient "Out of Scope", American Vanguard forced the project team to look at solutions involving formulation changes or delivery methods that would not adversely affect the effectiveness of the active ingredient. But by inhibiting run off, the new product would be far more environmentally friendly. More land could be used for banana plantations. Result: Risk of run-off would be eliminated and banana production/plantation would be increased.

As you go through the Value Innovation Process you should periodically revisit the project goals and objectives and make sure you are on track. There will be times you may have to refine the project objective based on what you uncover in the 1st Round of Contextual Interviews.

AmVac uncovered a new opportunity when they interviewed Plantation Managers and Superintendents. This opportunity will result in 20x more unit sales than a modified nematocide. AmVac continued with the nematocide project and also launched a new project to bring the new fungicide to fruition.

Using the template we created above, we will define the overall goals and objectives for 3 projects and generate the appropriate detail to illustrate how it works. Using a facilitator and a Mind Mapping software subject matter expert, you will find the process is fun and moves very quickly. The objective is to focus the team on the defined goal, knowing that it is very likely the goal and objectives will be revised after Step 4 of the Value Innovation Process. At this stage you do not know what the Most Important Customer's unmet needs are.

Company	Business Type	Most Important Customer	Project name
FoldedPak, Inc.	B2B and B2C	➢ Assumed to be Distributors who sell to manufacturers	ExpandOS™ (an environmentally friendly packaging material)
Net sales, >$5B In business for >30y	B2B or B2C	Internal to the company – The BUs	NexGen Performance Appraisal Process
Fortune 100	B2B	Individuals purchasing products and services for their BU	Purchasing Process Simplification

We selected FoldedPak because despite the apparent potential of its ExpandOS product line, the company had spent $7million of venture capital and was going nowhere. The business needed to go under the surgeon's knife to fix its latent problems.

Figure 1: ExpandOS was invented in 2003. Once the package is sealed, the serrated edges lock the pyramids in place so contents in the package do not move in transit. (The pyramid has a 3.2cm x 3.2cm Base and stands 3.5cm high)

Figure 2: The original machine was installed at the pack out station at the end of a production line. They were used about 10% of the time and machine reliability was poor.

<table>
<tr><td colspan="2">Project Name: ExpandOS</td></tr>
<tr><td colspan="2">Project Champion: Managing Partner of Duart Capital LLC and FoldedPak Interim CEO</td></tr>
<tr><td colspan="2">Project Leader: Director of Product Development</td></tr>
<tr><td colspan="2">Overall Goal: Deliver ExpandOS's potential and turn FoldedPak around, or recommend the doors be closed</td></tr>
<tr><td colspan="2">Objectives:

1. Examine key aspects of the FoldedPak's business:
o How is the company going to market? How is the product priced? Who are the primary customers? How is the product being used and how does it perform?
o How is the product manufactured? How much does it cost? What is the reliability of the machines that produce ExpandOS from scored and punched cardboard feedstock?
o How effective are FoldedPak's and its distributors' sales forces?
2. Analyze the output from 1 above, define options for substantially improving performance and develop plans for the paths forward. Make recommendations on what to implement, when.
3. Develop Value Chains for ExpandOS and identify the Most Important Customers
4. If it is apparent that FoldedPak has not identified its Most Important Customer(s) correctly, define the adjustments required in marketing and sales and implement same.
5. Meet with the VCs to review the outputs from 1 through 4. Agree on the path forward.</td></tr>
<tr><td>Project Start Date: Now</td><td>Targeted Complete Date: 1 month to complete the first four Steps of the Value Innovation Process</td></tr>
</table>

Expense Budget: Not to exceed $100,000 for out of pocket expenses	**Advisory Group:** VCs
Project Team Members: A 4 person team selected from manufacturing, sales, marketing and product development	
What's in Scope?: ➢ Considering B2C as well as B2B ➢ Shipping finished product to customers	**What's out of Scope?:** ➢ Major product redesign

The following two examples look at support groups within a company whose Most Important Customers are within the company.

NexGen Performance Assessment Process

This company has been in business for >30 years and annual net sales of > $5B. The company recognized its' existing performance appraisal process was outdated and ineffective, even though it uses 360 feedback. It was not helping deliver greater value to its external Most Important Customers. Most of all, the business unit heads thought the process was too complex, consumed too much time, created little value and, in many cases, drove the wrong behaviors. The consensus: "There must be a better way to do this."

One person in the management team was inspired by Ricardo Semler (1-2). For nearly 25 years, Ricardo Semler, CEO of Brazil-based Semco, has encouraged his employees to set their own hours, wages and even choose their own IT. The result has been increased productivity, long-term loyalty and phenomenal growth.

<table>
<tr><td colspan="2">Project Name: NexGen Performance Assessment Process</td></tr>
<tr><td colspan="2">Project Champion: CEO</td></tr>
<tr><td colspan="2">Project Leader: VP, Human Resources (reports to the COO)</td></tr>
<tr><td colspan="2">Overall Goal: Develop a new Performance Assessment Process that drives delivering value to the company's internal and external Most Important Customers</td></tr>
<tr><td colspan="2">Objectives:

1. Address and eliminate or reduce the challenges and problems identified by the business unit heads with the existing appraisal process
2. Address and eliminate the challenges and problems identified by people whose performance has been appraised using the existing appraisal process
3. Improve the quality of the process and the outcomes (needs to be defined and agreed to) by an order of magnitude.
4. Reduce the time to carry out the existing process by at least 50%
5. Reduce the cycle time to complete the appraisal process by at least 50%
6. Develop a set of Value Curve with Metrics templates for different functional areas and job levels that can be customized by supervisors/managers for use within their group
7. Use the individual's Value Curve with Metrics and his/her supervisor's Value Curve with Metrics to discuss, and agree on, what and how the individual can deliver greater value to the company and their boss.
8. Define how the individual and boss negotiate and agree on a "To Be" Value Curve that defines expectations on both the individual's and supervisor's performance over the next 12 months.</td></tr>
<tr><td>Project Start Date: Now</td><td>Targeted Complete Date: 3 months from the start date</td></tr>
<tr><td>Expense Budget: Not to exceed $350,000</td><td>Advisory Group: The COO and all BU heads</td></tr>
</table>

Project Team Members: A group of 5 (minimum) to 7 (Maximum) people, agreed to by the BU heads, who will be dedicated to the project team and collocated at company HQs.	
What's in Scope?: ➢ Benchmarking other companies ➢ Contextually interviewing supervisors at the manager, director, VP and "C" level ➢ Contextually interviewing individuals with 1-5, 5-10, 10-15, 15-20 and >20 years experience in the company ➢ Sharing the outcomes of the Contextual Interviews with all associates ➢ Sharing Value Curve with Metrics templates with associates	**What's out of Scope?:** ➢ Modifying the existing performance appraisal process ➢ Purchasing a system/package from a vendor

Increase productivity and reduce time purchasing standard items

This Fortune 100 company operates in more than 100 countries. It grew organically and through acquisition. Because there are different work processes and workflows in each business unit, as well as different software packages to support purchasing the business units are incompatible when ordering standard items. Unfortunately the company was not able to benefit from the economies of scale that accrue when large quantities of goods and services are purchased.

<table>
<tr><td colspan="2">Project Name: Purchasing Process Simplification (PPS)</td></tr>
<tr><td colspan="2">Project Champion: Chief Information Officer</td></tr>
<tr><td colspan="2">Project Leader: VP Controller</td></tr>
<tr><td colspan="2">Overall Goal: Develop a new process that will allow individuals from all BUs to purchase from an online company catalog, products and services from approved vendors, where pricing and terms are defined. Purchasing is not involved in these purchasing activities.</td></tr>
<tr><td colspan="2">Objectives:
1. Identify the products and services that should be included in the on line catalog
2. Determine the annual spend on these products and services using the current processes and estimate the cost savings that would accrue using a standardized process that could be used by individuals in all BUs
3. Define what value is being delivered to individuals today with the existing processes and what the new process must deliver.
4. Make recommendations on "How" to deliver the "What."</td></tr>
<tr><td>Project Start Date: Now</td><td>Targeted Complete Date: 6 months from the start date</td></tr>
<tr><td>Expense Budget: Out of pocket expense not to exceed $250,000 (Salaries and benefits of the team members are covered by their BUs)</td><td>Advisory Group: Directors of Purchasing from three large and three small BUs</td></tr>
<tr><td>Project Team Members:3 assistant purchasing managers and 3 IT managers familiar with the work processes and workflows used in purchasing, selected and agreed to by the BUs represented on the</td><td></td></tr>
</table>

Advisory Group.	
What's in Scope?: ➢ Recommending the purchase of an off the shelf software package which can be customized by the company's IT group ➢ Recommending spending authorization levels ➢ Contextually interviewing: ○ BU heads ○ Three groups of individuals who purchase <$50,000, $50,000 to $250,000 and >$250,000 of products and services a year that are not purchasing agents ○ Purchasing agents	**What's out of Scope?:** ➢ Developing a custom solution with an external vendor

As you can see from these examples, the use of a template will focus the "team". This is just an example. Use it to customize your own template. We cannot emphasize enough that the 10 Step Value Innovation Process needs to start from a position of clarity and focus. When the overall goal is determined and the objectives are set, the path forward is determined. We must re-emphasize, as the team progresses through Steps 2, 3 and 4 of the Value Innovation Process, the original project will probably need to be revised, refined, or even killed. Even if the project is killed, it could be replaced by a new project with a new goal and set of objectives. The 10 Step Value Innovation Process will continue to unfold in the next chapters.

Next Steps:

1. Take a current project and review the goals and objectives. Do those goals and objectives make sense?
2. Make sure you have a project champion, project leader and team.
3. Review "What is in Scope" and "What is Out of Scope" and make sure the direction is consistent with your organization's strategic direction.
4. Make sure this project is consistent with the company's mission and strategic direction.

Takeaways:

1. It is critically important to provide as much detail upfront to the project team as possible. Typically the project will be completed in 3 months. The team does not need to be coming back for redirection. It consumes time.
2. Make sure the project that you run through the Value Innovation Process is defined. Also make sure that the product and/or service development projects that you currently have in your project portfolio are defined.
3. Make sure the project in the Value Innovation Process has an appropriate project definition that is still consistent with the project. If it no longer makes sense, kill the project and start a new one, or refine the definition.
4. Make sure "What's in Scope" and "What's Out of Scope" is clearly defined and understood by the project team.

CHAPTER 3

"Your direct customer may not be your Most Important Customer"

Clay Christensen

Value Innovation Process Step #2:

Define the Value Chain (or Value Web) and Identify Your Most Important Customer(s)

Value Innovation is "Delivering exceptional value to the most important customer in the value chain, all the time, every time." To deliver exceptional value to that Most Important Customer, the Value Chain must be defined. After you have developed your Value Chain you identify the Most Important Customer by using The Three Questions and the Three Question Template.

Christensen and Raynor were the first to recognize that your direct customer may not be the most important customer (1). "A company's channel [value chain] includes not just wholesale distributors and retail stores, but any entity that adds value to, or creates value around, the company's product {or service} as it wends its way towards the hands of the end user.....there needs to be symmetry of motivation across the entire chain of entities that add value to the product {or service} on its way to the end consumer. If your product or service does not help all of those entities do their fundamental jobs better.....then you will struggle to succeed."

This is critical in determining your Most Important Customer. Once you understand this fact, you will view the world differently. Example: You are a chemical company seeing your direct customers as your most important customer. You focus your time and effort working with the customer's purchasing staff. You are struggling to succeed. Yes, your sales force needs to call on purchasing to close business, but there is a clear distinction between the goal of purchasing and your most important customer's unmet, unarticulated needs.

What is a Value Chain?

The Value Chain identifies each company, organization, or individual involved in a buying, selling, or using transaction between you and the ultimate end user. The Value Chain starts with your product or service and ends when the final product or service is used.

The value chain as we define it should not be confused with Michael Porter's definition (2): The value chain categorizes the generic value-adding activities of an organization. The main activities respectively are: inbound logistics, production, outbound logistics, sales and marketing, maintenance. These activities are supported by: administrative infrastructure management, human resources management, R&D, and procurement.

Value chains can be long or short: If we look at Archer Daniels Midland's or Cargill's corn businesses, their value chains are very long. There are many steps from planting the corn to its arrival at the dinner table. From fertilizing, harvesting, processing, warehousing, distribution, retail sales, etc. to eventually finding its' way to the dining table, many customers are involved. If you are a manufacturer of fixtures, racks, and refrigerated cases used by supermarkets and mass merchants (e.g., Hussmann, the value chain is very short (Manufacturer, Supermarket, and the consumer who removes products from those cases).

If you are in the consumer packaged goods industry (e.g., Avon Products, Colgate Palmolive, Henkel, Kao, Kimberley-Clark, L'Oréal, Procter and Gamble, Reckitt Benckiser, S. C. Johnson and Unilever), what everybody defines as B2C, likewise your Value Chain is very short. You sell to mass merchants and supermarkets who sell your products to the consumer.

Identifying the Most Important Customer

Once you have developed your Value Chain, you use the 3 Questions and the Three Question Template to identify the Most Important Customer.

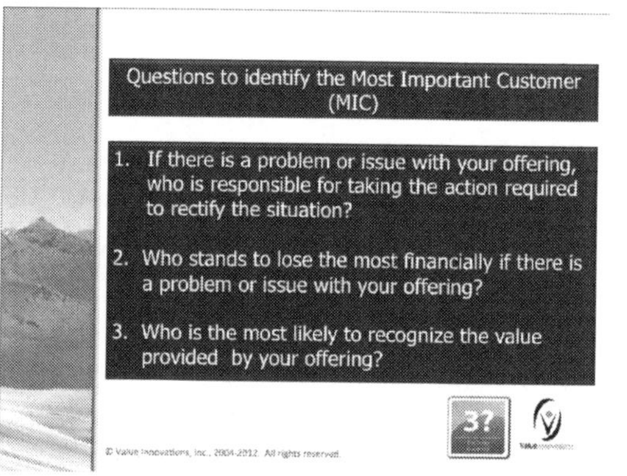

It is important to understand that the Most Important Customer could be a user of your product or service. They may not buy it, or sell it.

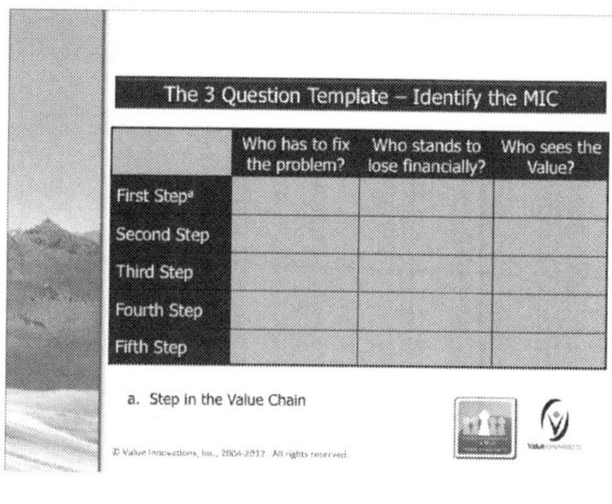

As you can see from the graphic on the front cover of this book, The Most Important Customer is central to the Value Innovation Process. We present six case studies to show you how to identify the Most Important Customer using Value Chains, The 3 Questions and the 3 Question Template. We start with the simplest case study. Thereafter, each case study builds in complexity.

	Business	Business Type
1	RE/MAX International ➢ A new business model in the purchase and sale of commercial and residential real estate ➢ Founded in 1973	B2B and B2C
2	Fast Moving Consumer Packaged Goods (FMCPG) ➢ Branded products and Private Label	B2C (B2B)
3	Fibers used in armament systems ➢ Vehicles and personal body armor	B2B and B2G
4	Replacement Auto Parts ➢ Europe & the US	B2B
5	Emergency Vehicles ➢ Police Cars ➢ Ford Interceptor and Carbon Motors E-	B2G
6	FoldedPak's ExpandOS ➢ Environmentally friendly packaging material ➢ Venture capital funded company founded in 2004	B2B and B2C

B2B, Business to Business; B2C, Business to Consumer; B2G, Business to Government

1. The Value Chain for the purchase and sale of real estate (B2B and B2C)

RE/MAX International is the largest real estate company in the world based on the value of the commercial and residential properties sold. RE/MAX's value chain is a very simple one (see Figure 3).

Figure 3: The RE/MAX International Value Chain

RE/MAX's business model is fundamentally different from that of its primary competitors, Prudential and Century 21. RE/MAX does not set realtor commission rates or transaction terms; they leave that to the Sales Affiliate. The Sales Affiliate keeps 95% of the commission (5% goes to the franchisee) but the Sales Affiliate pays REMAX a monthly fee for office support, a computer and phone, leads, peer experience and blanket advertizing (both print and TV).

RE/MAX's immediate customers are their 7,000 Franchisees. The Franchisees provide offices, with Sales

Affiliates working out of those offices and the Sales Affiliates interface directly with the customer who is buying and selling real estate. Who is the Most Important Customer in the value chain for RE/MAX International (See Figure 4)?

Figure 4: RE/MAX International's Most Important Customer

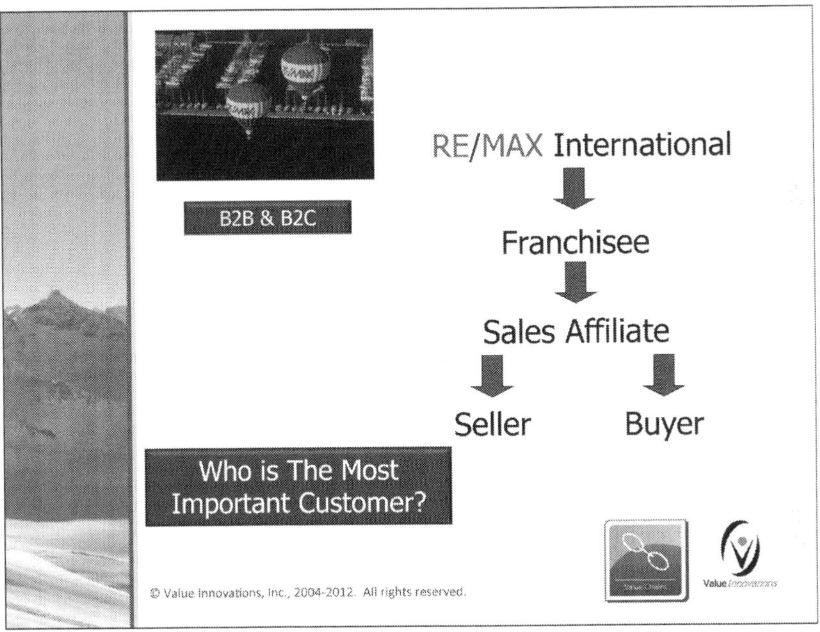

It is the Sales Affiliate who sees the value, who suffers financially if they do not close deals and they fix problems with the deals that can occur literally on a daily basis. The key metric that the senior leadership team looks at to measure the health of their business every morning is, "how many new Sales Affiliates signed contracts to join the RE/MAX team yesterday?"

2. Value Chain for Fast Moving Consumer Packaged Goods (FMCPG) Companies (B2B and B2C)

With annual net sales of $80B, Procter and Gamble is the world's largest Fast Moving Consumer Packaged Goods Company. They have 50 brands, 24 of them generating $1B in revenues a year. Their largest brand is Tide (annual sales, $4B) and their largest customer is Walmart. Walmart represents about 25% of P&G's annual sales.

The Value Chain (Figure 5) and the Three Question Template (Figure 6) for Fast Moving Consumer Packaged Goods companies are very simple.

Figure 5: Fast Moving Consumer Packaged Goods Value Chain

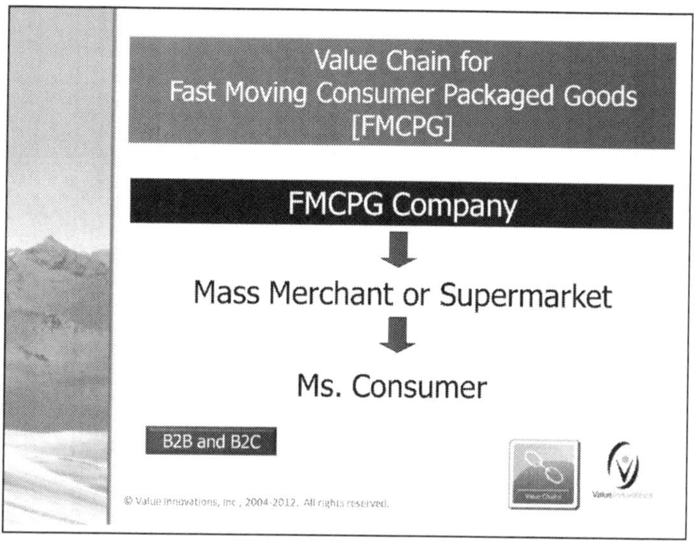

Figure 6: Fast Moving Consumer Packaged Goods Three Question Template

Fast Moving Consumer Packaged Goods
The 3 Question Template

	Who has to fix the problem?	Who loses financially?	Who sees the Value?
Mass Merchant or Supermarket	X	X	X
Department Merchandiser		X	X
Purchasing			Possibly
Operations	-	-	-
Distribution	-	-	-
Marketing	X		X
Ms Consumer	Possibly	X	X

Ms. Consumer is the Fast Moving Consumer Packaged Goods Most Important Customer. That said, Ms Consumer comes in many forms and the Fast Moving Consumer Packaged Goods companies have to focus on the demographic and geography they are targeting: Age, household income, country, urban or country, ethnic background and language spoken all come into play. They have to be considered when figuring out the Zeroth, First and Second Moments of Truth Value Curves with Metrics (see Chapter 4). This is true whether you are selling your own brands or you are a company supplying private label products.

Within the Mass Merchant or Supermarket, it is important to understand who your target person is. It is not acceptable to be talking to and interfacing with just anybody at WalMart, Carrefour, or Tesco. From the Three Question template, it looks as though it should be the department merchandisers. They have the responsibility for maximizing the gross margin/unit floor area and gross margin/unit shelf space (gross margin \$, £, or €/annum per square foot or per square meter) for every one of their stores. If you can help them maximize their gross margin, they will listen.

3. Value Chain for fibers used in armament systems (B2B and B2G)

Manufacturer X produces fibers used in clothing and vehicle armament systems. Their fiber offers 4 times more protection performance than Kevlar but they have been unsuccessful selling their product. Why? The Value Chain tells the story.

- Fiber manufacturer sells fibers to fabricators.
- Fabricators use the fibers to produce mats or weaves.
- Fabricators sell their mats or weaves to a component manufacturer who produces a fiber-reinforced panel that goes inside the door of a Humvee.
- Component manufacturers sell those parts to a vehicle manufacturer who in turn, sells vehicles to the military.
- Soldiers in those vehicles depend on the components to protect them from IED's, bullets, etc. The Value Chain is shown in Figure 7:

Figure 7 : Value Chain for the Mfr of Fibers used in Vehicle Armor Systems

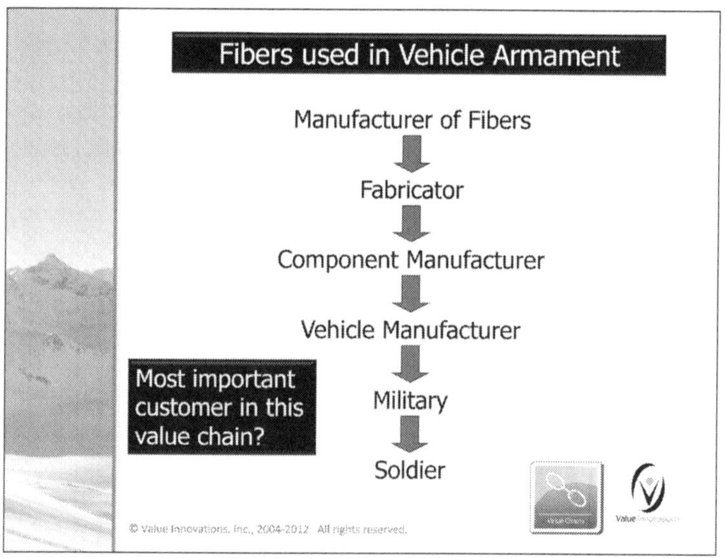

Using The 3 Questions and The Three Question template (see Figure 8), the company concluded the Military is the Most Important Customer. Some argue that it is the soldier. After all, it is his or her life that is on the line. We agree, but the troops must work with what the Military provides to them.

Figure 8: The Three Question Template for the Manufacturer of Fibers used in Vehicle Armament Systems

Fibers used in Vehicle Armament

The 3 Question Template – Identify the MIC

	Who has to fix the problem?	Who stands to lose financially?	Who sees the Value?
Fabricator			
Component Mfr			
Vehicle Mfr	X		
US Military	X	X	X
Soldier		X	X

There are military specifications for fibers used in vehicle protection systems. However, these specifications have not kept up with the reality of today's warfare. Both Kevlar and Manufacturer X's fiber meet the current specifications. The entities at the top of the Value Chain focused on maximizing their margins rather than providing greater protection to soldiers.

The fiber manufacturer was making a major mistake by selling to the purchasing agents at the fabricator. By default, the fabricator was making the buy/sell decision using the following decision making process: Does it meet the Military Specs? Yes.

Which is the lowest cost product? Kevlar, so that is the product we will purchase. As long as Manufacturer X continued to talk to fabricator purchasing agents, they would not sell their product.

This resulted in the company with the better performing fiber selling no product because of cost (4X that or Kevlar on a price/lb basis). Are they providing the best protection for the soldier sitting in their Humvees? No. The U.S. Military is the Most Important Customer. The U.S. Military is trying to keep soldiers alive. The Military suffers when there's a problem. As a result, they see the value in the better performing fiber. Cost is not the issue. The military cares about keeping their soldiers alive.

So what should Manufacture X do? Meet with the Military and get them involved in discussions with the fabricators. They need to sell value: "Our product keeps soldiers alive."

4. Value chain for the Automotive Replacement Parts business (B2B)

The auto parts company could be a manufacturer of any one of the following: alternators, belts, gas caps, hoses, hub caps, mufflers, wheels, windows, etc. This is a several hundred billion dollar market, employing more than 600,000 people in the US. Robert Bosch is the world's largest auto parts manufacturer. In the US, Delphi and Visteon, spin-outs from GM and Ford are the market share leaders. These companies, and many other Tier 1 and 2 suppliers, sell to the OEM's at very low margins. They make much higher margins on their replacement parts business.

In the US, the manufacturer sells to a distributor (e.g., NAPA and CarQuest), the distributor sells to a jobber and/or auto parts store. These are typically very small companies that service a small part of a city or town. The jobber, or parts store, sells to auto dealers and repair shops in their area. Ultimately you, the consumer, buy the replacement part when the repair shop fixes your car (See Figure 9).

Figure 9: Replacement Auto Parts Value Chains

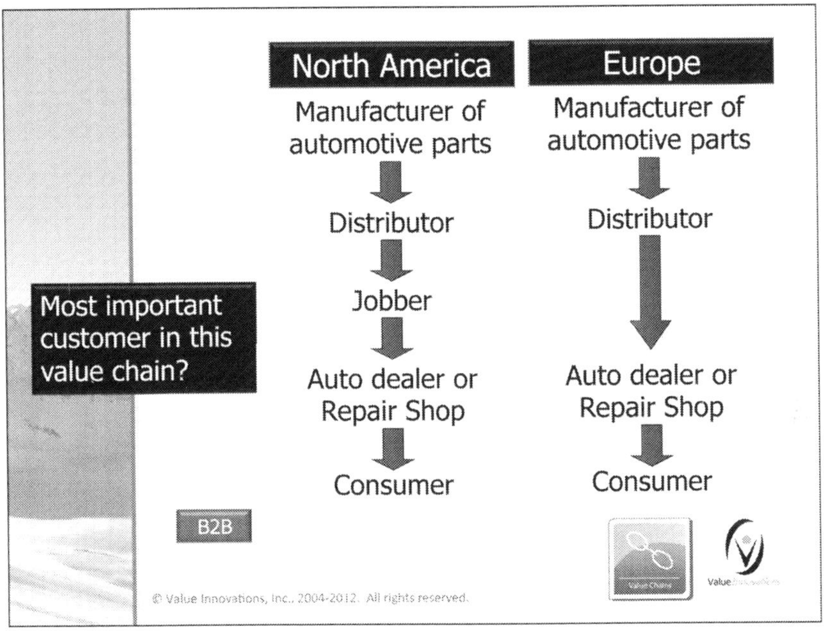

The Value Chain in Europe differs from that in the USA. The countries are geographically smaller than the US. Therefore distributors are able to ship parts by truck overnight directly to the auto dealer or repair shop, eliminating Jobbers.

Using The Three Question template below, (see Figure 10) look at each member of the Value Chain, ask The Three Questions and place an "X" in the table where the answer is "Yes". Place a "P" in the table where you're unsure or the answer is "Possible". Leave the cell blank if the answer is "No."

Figure 10: The Three Question Template for Auto Replacement Parts

The 3 Question Template – Identify the MIC

	Who has to fix the problem?	Who stands to lose financially?	Who sees the Value?
Distributor			
Jobber			
Auto Dealer	X	X	X
Repair Shop	X	X	X
Consumer			

Conclusion: The auto dealer and repair shop are the Most Important Customers in this value chain. Why? If there is a problem with the part that is needed for your car, it is the Auto Repair shop or Auto Dealers job to fix it. If they have to replace the part multiple times because the wrong part is delivered, they lose financially. The auto parts manufacturer will replace the wrong/faulty part at no cost but they will not cover the labor to replace the part multiple times. The Auto Repair shop/Auto Dealer sees the value. The part fits, it works, the problem is solved, and the customer is happy. If it is a belt or hose, the repair shop does not care if it is manufactured by Gates, Veyance or Dayco. They do not care about belts or hoses that last for 100,000 miles or the color of the belt and probably do not care about the price. Their position, "Just help me take care of my customer, now."

There are >300,000 auto repair shops and approximately 15,000 auto dealerships in the United States. The auto parts manufacturer's goal should be to deliver exceptional value to repair shops and auto dealers.

This example is unusual. It is very clear who the Most Important Customer is. In our experience: It is rare that you get a clear-cut answer to The Three Questions, i.e., finding one group with 3 Xs but you will always find a group with 2 Xs.

When there could be two Most Important Customers we advise you to treat them both as Most Important Customers as you move forward into Steps 3 and 4 of The Value Innovation Process. Once you start Contextual Interviewing in Step 4 it will become very clear who the Most Important Customer is.

5. Value Chain for Emergency Vehicles – Ford Interceptor and Carbon Motors E-7 Police Cars (B2G)

Carbon Motors was formed in 2003 by William Santana Li, the ex VP of Engineering at the Ford Motor Company.

We do not believe Carbon Motors used Value Innovation methodology and tools but it is a very interesting case study. The E-7 police car, built from the ground up, features light weight body parts, standard police car components, and a BMW turbo diesel engine Figure 11). These translate into lower operating and maintenance costs, higher fuel efficiency, increased performance (maximum speed is 160 mph) compared to a police car converted from a passenger vehicle (Ford Crown Victoria Interceptor, Dodge Challenger, BMW 3 Series, or a Volvo).

Figure 11: The Carbon Motors E-7 Police car

Carbon Motors sells to State and Local Governments (see the Value Chain shown Figure 12). Detail for Local Government is provided on the right hand side of the Value Chain. Admin, Purchasing, Operations and Maintenance groups in the City and County Sheriff's Departments are involved with the E-7. Communications (dispatch) and the officer are directly involved in the control and operation of the police car.

Figure 12: Value Chain for Carbon Motors

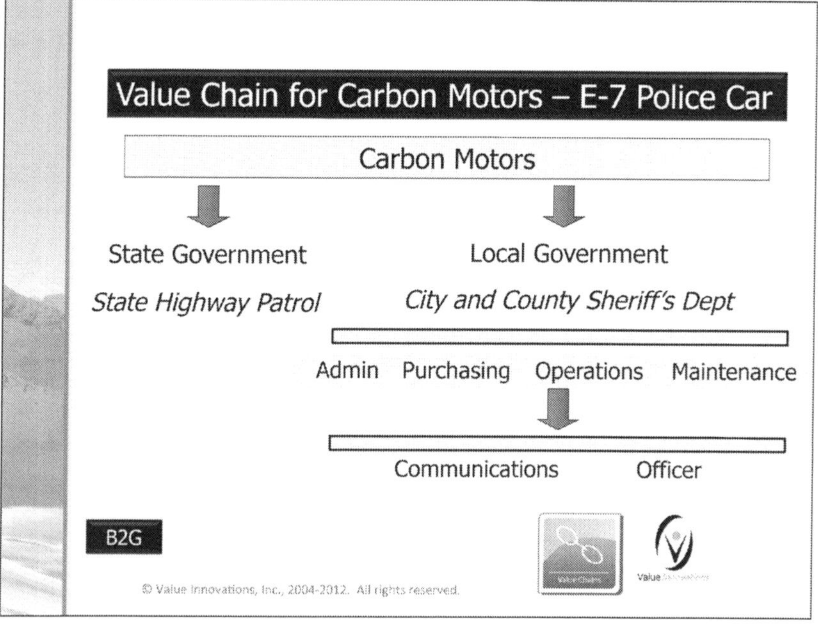

The Three Question Template for the Carbon Motors E-7 Police Car is shown in Figure 13.

Figure 13: Carbon Motors Three Question Template

Carbon Motors E-7 Police car:
The 3 Question Template

City and County Sheriff's Dept	Who has to fix the problem?	Who loses financially?	Who sees the Value?
Administration	X	X	X
Purchasing			X
Operations	XX	XX	XX
Maintenance	XX		
Communications			X
Officer	Possibly		X

Operations is the Most Important Customer. Patrol officers driving the E-7 and communicating with dispatch are key influencers. Patrol officers love the E-7!

6. Value Chains for FoldedPak's ExpandOS (B2B and B2C)

ExpandOS is a breakthrough product. It is a recyclable packaging material alternative to bubble wrap, foam in place and peanuts. During the period 2004 to 2009, FoldedPak assumed the Value Chain for ExpandOS was as shown in Figure 14 and that their Most Important Customer was their direct customer. These erroneous conclusions cost FoldedPak a lot of money and time. $7 million were invested from 2004-2009.

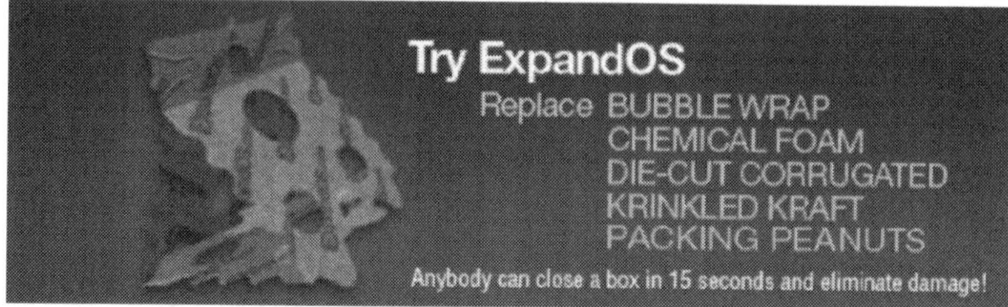

Brad Fehn, managing partner at Duart Capital LLCwas called in by the Venture Capital investors to analyze the situation at FoldedPak and make a recommendation on what to do. One option was to close the doors. Brad, using the Value Innovation Process, concluded FoldedPak had miscued and that their Most Important Customer was not the Distributor. All the distributors wanted was lower product prices and a lower cost for the equipment required to produce ExpandOS. They focused on all manufacturers. They were not targeting manufacturers of high value added, fragile products who would recognize, and pay for, a packaging material that would eliminate breakage in shipping.

Figure 14: Value Chain for FoldedPak, 2004 - 2009.

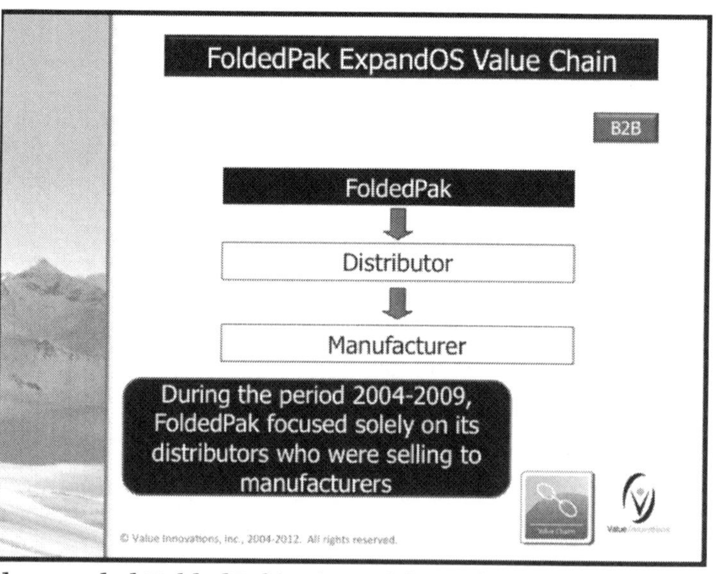

Brad expanded FoldedPak's view of the Value Chain (see Figure 15).

Figure 15: Revised Value Chain for FoldedPak

FoldedPak ExpandOS Value Chain
B2B and B2C
FoldedPak
Distributor
Mfr
Retailer
Mfr
Retailer
Consumer
Consumer
The only Value Chain pursued by FoldedPak in 2004-2009

The Most Important Customer on the B2B side was the manufacturer of high value added, fragile products. ExpandOS eliminates breakage! It cannot effectively compete with Styrofoam peanuts in the void fill application, it is too expensive.

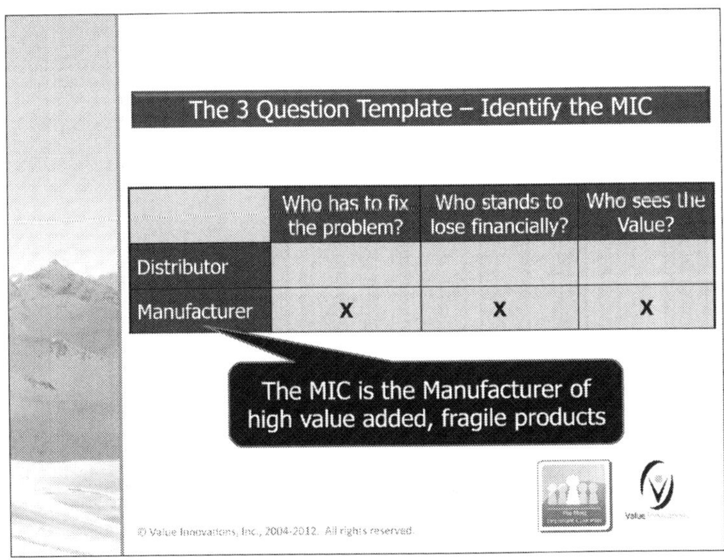

The Most Important Customer on the B2C side was the consumer.

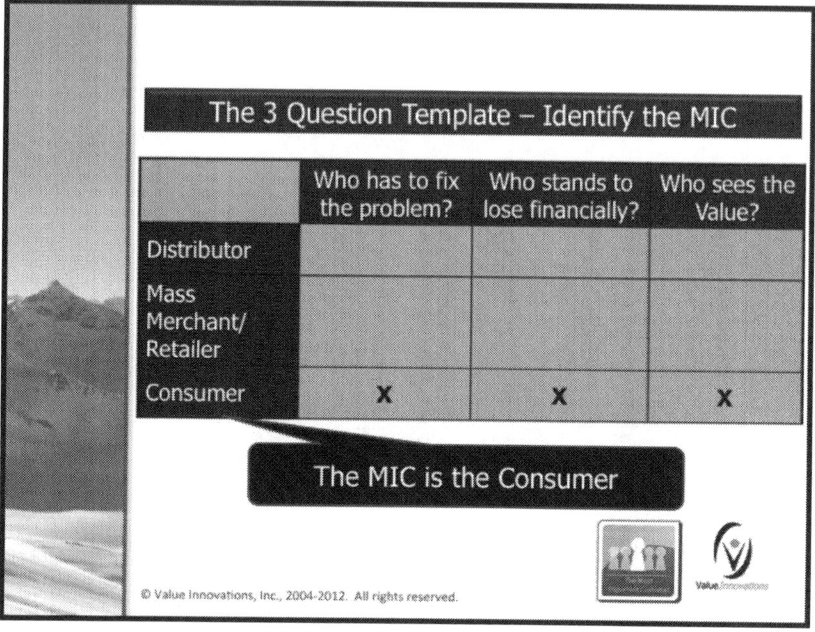

With the expanded view of the Value Chain (see Figure 16), FoldedPak was able to correctly identify its Most Important Customers and the company was on its way to a much brighter future.

Figure 16: FoldedPak ExpandOS Value Chain – 2009 to present

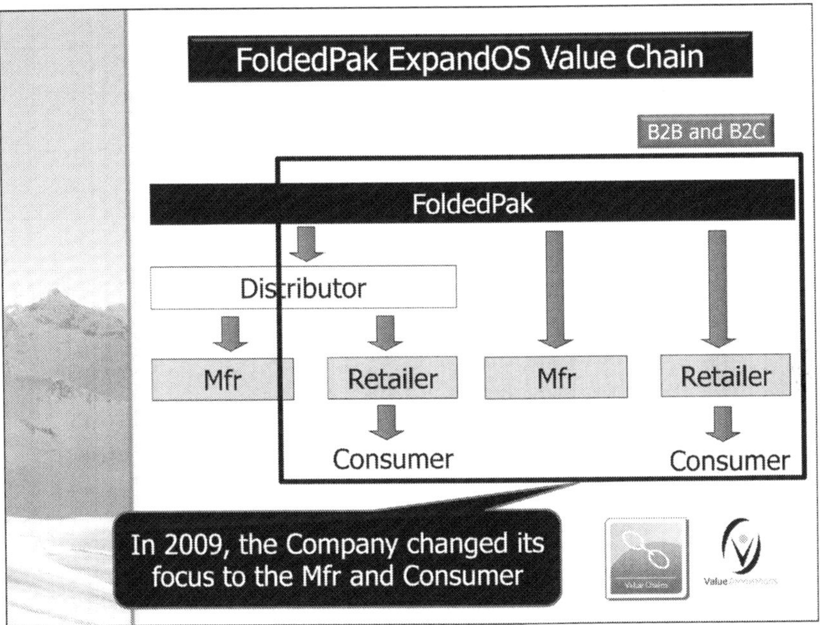

Who is the Most Important Customer within the Most Important Customer?

We have shown examples to help you determine which entity within a Value Chain is the Most Important Customer. Once you have identified that Most Important Customer, can you go to any person in that organization? No. We saw in the Carbon Motors E-7 police car case the Most Important Customer within thc City and County Sherriff's Department was Operations. The example of a manufacturer of fixtures, cases, and refrigeration systems used in supermarkets and mass merchants is very short (see Figure 17).

FIGURE 17: Value Chain for a case and/or refrigerated case Manufacturer

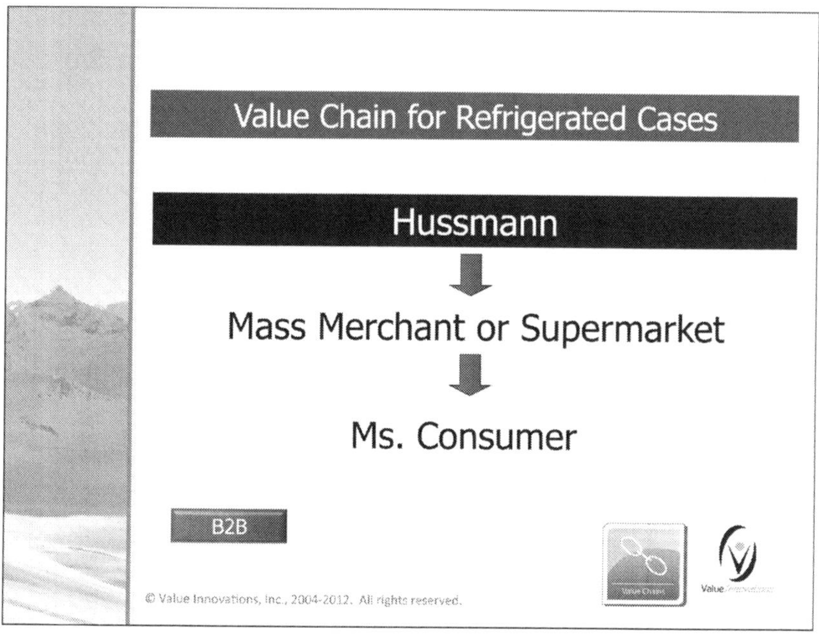

The Most Important Customer in the value chain is the Mass Merchant/Supermarket/Retailer. The question is, "Who is the Most Important Customer" within the Mass Merchant/Supermarket/Retailer? Who is the person who is the decision maker when it comes to delivering value on refrigerated systems and support services to ASDA, Carrefour, Morrisons, Safeway, Tesco, Wal-Mart, or Whole Foods?

There are many organizations within the mass merchant that have some involvement with refrigerated systems: Architects, Space Planners, Engineering, Store Management, Corporate Growth, Marketing, Department Merchandisers, Store Maintenance, Counter Clerks, Purchasing, etc. To have success, it is imperative to determine that Most Important Customer.

Use the same process employing the Three Questions and the Three Question Template (see Figure 18). Enjoy the following exercise and see how you do. Who is the Most

Important Customer within the Most Important Customer organization?

Figure 18: Three Question Template for Hussmann

Who is the Most Important Customer?

	Who has to fix the problem?	Who stands to lose financially?	Who sees the Value?
Architects			
Space Planners			
Engineering			
Store Management			
Corporate Growth			
Marketing			
Dept. Merchandisers			
Store Maintenance			
Counter Clerks			
Purchasing			

Identifying the Most Important Customer in your organization

If your primary role is to support other parts of your organization, i.e., you are a support group: Corporate Growth, Distribution and Logistics, Finance, IT, Human Resources, Purchasing, and Strategic Planning, etc., you need to identify your Most Important Customers too. You could assume they are the people or groups you support now but if it is not clear, pull out your organization chart, look at each group and ask yourself the Three Questions.

We used this approach on a project we were working on for the IT group of a Fortune 50 company and concluded it was the individuals who had P&L responsibility who were the Most Important Customers, not the people who were using the software. Making this change from users to BU heads made a huge difference. The unmet, unarticulated needs of users and

BU heads were totally different.

There are situations when a straight line Value Chain will not suffice. In these cases we recommend you use a Value Web. It takes into account the role of key influencers.

	**What is a Value Web and how is it different from a Value Chain?** Like the Value Chain, the Value Web identifies each company, organization, or individual involved in a buying, selling, or using the transaction between you and the ultimate end user. The difference between a Value Chain, the Value Web identifies, and takes into account, key influencers.

The Value Web takes into account organizations and bodies that are not involved in a buying, selling or using transaction but they have a major indirect influence on the product you sell, or the service(s) you provide. If you are in the pharmaceutical industry, the FDA has regulations that you must adhere to. Likewise in the chemical industry in the USA, OSHA and EPA may have regulations that impact what you do and how you do it. The FAA regulates the US airline industry, ICAO and IATA regulates the world's airlines, etc.

If you are a medical device company, and your products are used in hospitals, doctors' offices and surgicenters, these organizations have protocols and procedures in place that impact how your product is used in their facilities. It is highly unlikely that they will be Most Important Customers, but they probably are key influencers.

Number	Business Type	Business
1	B2B	Alcan Pharma Packaging ➢ Pharmaceutical Packaging
2	B2B and B2C	J&J, Smith and Nephew and Stryker ➢ Knee Replacements in India

1. Value Web for Pharmaceutical Packaging (B2B)

Alcan Pharmaceutical Packaging was working on a project to re-invent physician samples. Physician samples are unique because they bridge the gap from diagnosis to treatment, but they are still just drugs. They are often the first introduction to a potential treatment for a patient. If the sample the patient received from the physician is taken incorrectly the patient will never know if it might have worked. Drug samples are often treated as freebies and not treated seriously by patients. Alcan visited a number of Doctors' offices and found that due to small storage areas the packaging that contained the instructions on how to use the sample had been removed. Doctors unintentionally contributed to the "freebie" image by removing the packaging. Alcan wanted to understand the "job that the physician sample was hired to do" and what would help the patient take the right drug at the right time. There was an early realization that a straight line Value Chain could not capture the complexity of this situation. They used a Value Web (See Figure 19).

Figure 19: The Value Web for Alcan Pharmaceutical Packaging

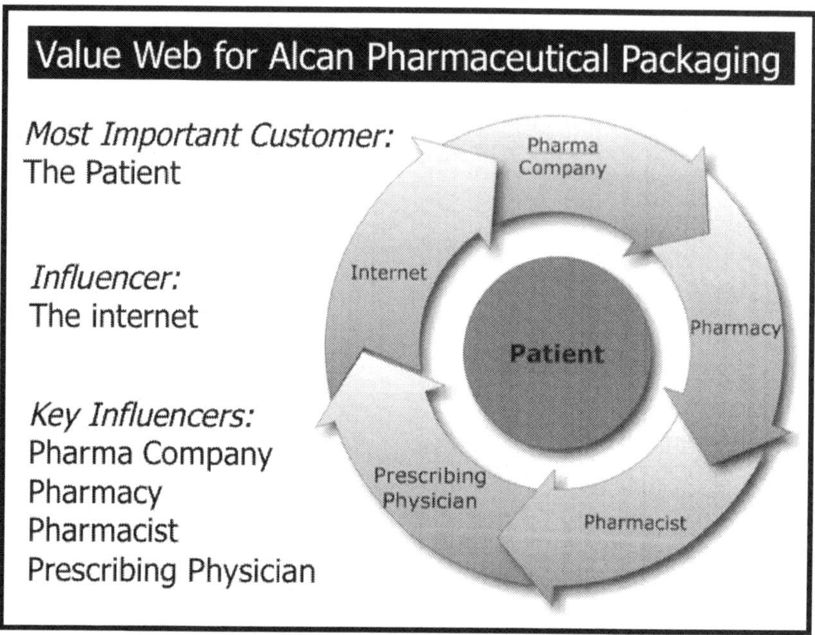

It was clear the Most Important Customer was the patient but there were multiple influencers in prescribing a drug and dispensing same. In the center of the Value Web is the patient (the Most Important Customer). In a great surprise to Alcan, they found patients relied not only on the doctor but pharmacists and the internet for information on the proposed treatment. Most drugs in North America are repackaged into plastic vials at the pharmacy. In Europe they are often in blister packaging designed by the manufacturer. The generic plastic vials in North America do not differentiate between treatments or help patients take their medication correctly. The value web enabled Alcan to observe a shift in influencers from the Pharma Brand Owner and Doctor to the Pharmacy. Pharmacies had been working to develop a way to differentiate their value to customers and had started to create distinct packaging that helped the patient take the right drug at the right time. Alcan interviewed influencers and patients. Patient interviews highlighted the role that the internet played in understanding their diagnosis and treatment. Insights to develop better packaging solutions for physician samples were drawn from the patients and the web of influencers.

2. Value Web for Knee Replacements in India (B2B and B2C)

Osteoarthritis is a significant problem in India. In 1 million more reported cases a year, 4 out of 5 people with osteoarthritis are women. Their osteoarthritis occurs in their knees. With this significant problem, in 2011, only 50,000 knee replacements were carried out in India. Why? The three major manufacturers supplying devices for this surgery direct their sales effort at the physician.

We looked at the Value Web for knee replacements in India (See Figure 20) and concluded the manufacturers are selling to the wrong person. Using the 3 questions (See Figure 21), it is clear the Most Important Customer is the Pre-Surgery Patient and the most significant key influencer is the Post-Surgery Patient. It is not the Physician. Why? Women overwhelmingly are afraid of the surgery, the pain and its outcome.

Figure 20: The Value Web for Knee Replacements in India

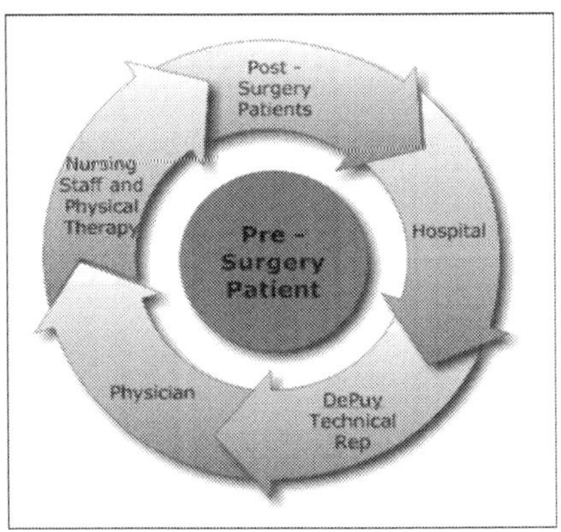

Figure 21: The Three Question Template for a Manufacturer of Replacement Knees in India

Knee Replacements in India: The 3 Question Template

	Who has to fix the problem?	Who loses financially?	Who sees the Value?
Hospital		Possibly	
Medical Device Tech Rep	X		
Physician	XX		
Operation Room Nursing Staff			X
Physical Therapist	XXX		
Pre Surgery Patient	X	X	X
Post Surgery Patient			X

There are two significant challenges for the manufacturers:

1. Access to the new cases of osteoarthritis, especially in remote villages in a country with a village population of more than 600 million.

2. To overcome their fears/perceptions about the operation:

   - Will I come out alive?
   - Will I be in a lot of pain during and after the surgery?
   - Will it be successful and will I be able to walk again?
   - How long will it take me to recover so I can go back to work?

Post surgery patients can answer these questions based on their actual experience. The Post-Surgery Patients are far more credible to the Pre-Surgery Patients than the physician.

Next Steps:

1. Take a current project and develop a Value Chain.

2. Use The Three Questions to identify the Most Important Customer.

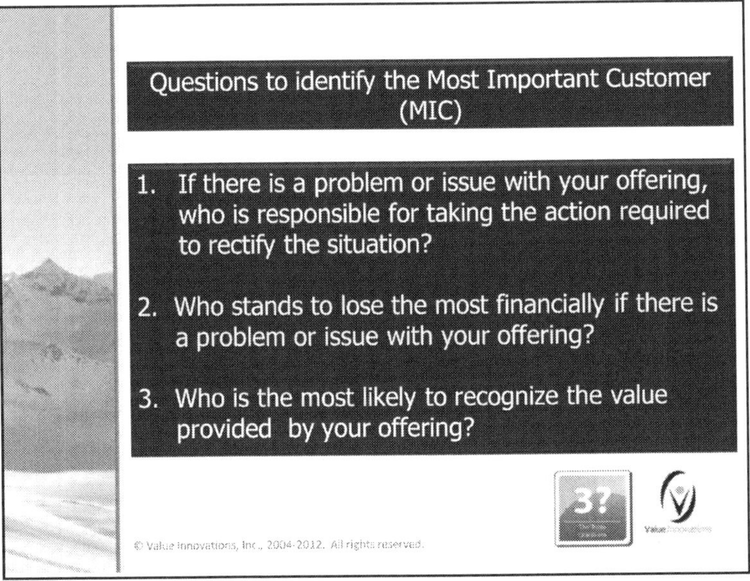

Question 1: If there is a problem or issue with your product or service, who is responsible for taking action required to rectify the situation?

Question 2: Who stands to lose most financially if there is a problem or issue with your product or service?

Question 3: Who is most likely to recognize the value provided by your product or service?

3. Summarize your findings in the following Template

The 3 Question Template

	Who has to fix the problem?	Who stands to lose financially?	Who sees the Value?
Your Company			

4. Are you interfacing with the right Most Important Customers? If not, what is the right course of action?

Stop the project and start over? _____

Kill the project? _____

Carry on regardless? _____

Takeaways:

1. Developing a Value Chain for each specific project is the most important first step. It is easy to do and takes very little time (<1h). This task identifies the Most Important Customer.
2. If there is a customer, develop a Value Chain.
3. Use The Three Questions and The Three Questions Template to identify the Most Important Customers in the Value Chain.
4. In our experience, there will always be two clear-cut answers to The Three Questions.
5. If it is not clear who the Most Important Customer is, there are two possible Most Important Customers, treat both as Most Important Customers.
6. In the world of B2B, our experience is that most of the time the direct customer is NOT the Most Important Customer.
7. Even in the world of B2C, most large companies will have to deal with an intermediary, e.g., The Fast Moving Consumer Packaged Goods with mass merchandisers, supermarkets, and other retailers. If you sell directly to the consumer, i.e., you own your own store, restaurant, or lemonade stand, then you are a true B2C business.
8. When the Most Important Customer is identified, it is important to determine the specific person within the company who is the Most Important Customer. Use The Three Questions to identify the Most Important Customer within the Most Important Customer.
9. If you have identified Purchasing or Strategic Sourcing as your Most Important Customer, start this process again. Your target is that person/organization that is focused on the value you can help bring to their Most Important Customer(s).
10. This process works very well even if your Most Important Customers are inside your organization.

CHAPTER 4

"A picture shows me at a glance what it takes dozens of pages of a book to expound."

Ivan Turgenev, Russian Writer, 1862

Value Innovation Process Step #3:

Develop "As Is" and "Best in Class" Value Curves with Metrics for Your Most Important Customer

A Value Curve with Metrics paints a clear picture (See below):

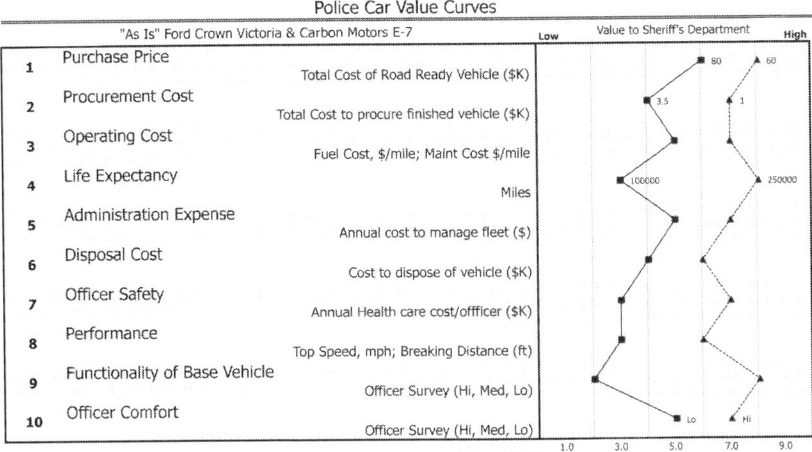

One PowerPoint slide captures the path to deliver exceptional value to the Most Important Customer in the Value Chain.

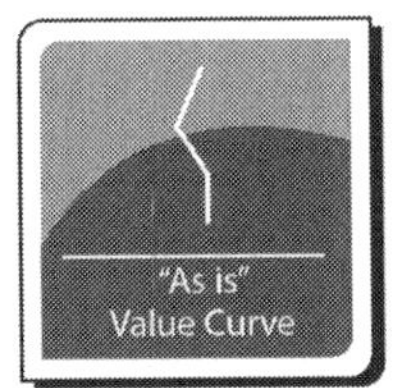

What is a Value Curve with Metrics?

View the Value Curve above.

The left side of the Value Curve lists the Elements of Performance in order of importance to the Most Important Customer. The first Element is the most important to the Most Important Customer. In aggregate these Elements define your product, service or offering.

The right side lists both values being delivered to the Most Important Customer for your current offering ("As Is" - if you have one) and "Best in Class" on a value scale (low on the left and high on the right). Each Element has a value.

What is an Element of Performance?

An Element of Performance is a capability or characteristic of your product, service or offering that is important to the Most Important Customer and can be performed/observed in a measurable way. Steve Shacher, EPMO, Chevron.

An Element of Performance is a succinct statement. It is not an objective, nor is it a feature/benefit, e.g., We are a Belgian brewery developing a new beer. One of the Elements of Performance is very likely to be Taste. It is not, Improve Taste – this is an objective. It is not Tastes Great – this is a feature. The "To Be" and "As Is" Value Curves with Metrics will tell us what we need to do with taste to deliver greater value to the consumer.

In the world of B2B there is just one Value Curve with Metrics for the Most Important Customer. In B2C, e.g., Fast Moving Consumer Packaged Goods and Consumer Electronics there are three Value Curves with metrics for the Most Important Customer (The Zeroth, the First and the Second Moments of Truth). We go into more detail on these Moments of Truth in the Novamin – Oravive toothpaste case study in this chapter. Let's take an example and look at the key points of a Value Curve using a police car.

You will recall Carbon Motors' E-7 police car was an example in Chapter 3. The E-7 is, at printing, not available, so the sheriff's and police departments around the world still purchase standard production cars and the convert them into police cars. They can also purchase a Volvo V70 police car that is a factory conversion.

Volvo V70 Police Car – Factory Built, 2008

Strathclyde Police BMW 5 Series Police Car, 2006

In the US the Ford Crown Victoria Interceptor has been the car of choice. It was first produced as a sedan in 1977. Production ceased in 2011. At the time of writing, there were about 450,000 Ford Crown Victoria Police cars in service in the US.

In Chapter 2 we concluded the Sheriff's/police Department

was the Most Important Customer and operations is the Most Important Customer within the Sheriff's Department.

New York Police Department Ford Crown Victoria Police Car, 2001

Here is the "As Is" Value Curve with Metrics for the Ford Crown Victoria police car for the Sheriff's Department (See Figure 20):

- The Elements of Performance are listed on the left hand side (See call out A);
- The Elements are listed in rank order (See call out B);
- Each Element has a metric (See call out C) and
- The value delivered to the Sheriff's Department by the Ford Crown Victoria is shown on the right (See call out D).

A 1 to 9 scale is used to define the value (1 is low value on the left; 9 is high value on the right) delivered on each Element to the Sheriffs' Department. Note that an absolute value for each metric is provided, e.g., Total Cost of the Road Ready Vehicle, $K – 80, i.e., its' $80,000; Procurement Cost, $K – 3.5; Life Expectancy, miles – 100,000.

We have developed a software package, Slalom®, that allows you to easily construct these Value Curves with Metrics. They provide the level of detail that you need and senior management wants to see.

Figure 20: The Police Car Value Curve with Metrics

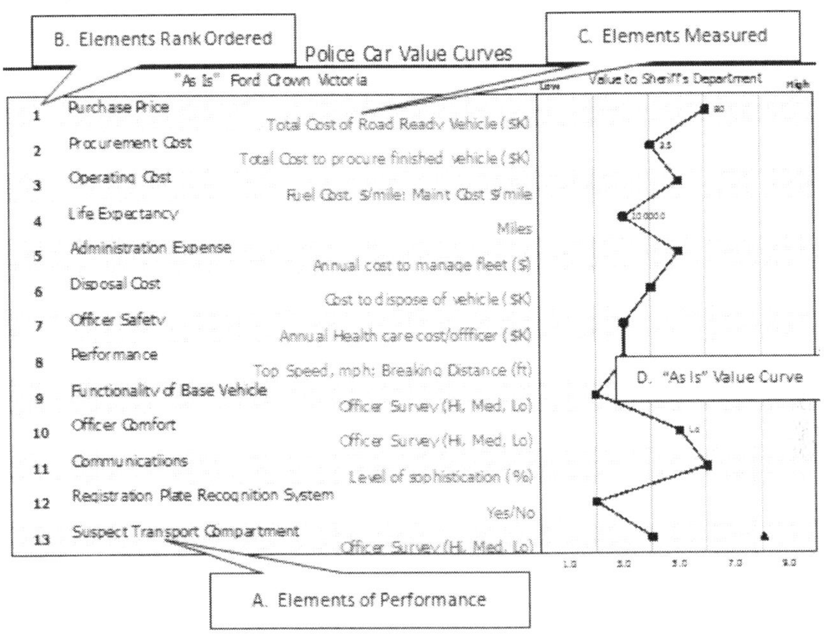

Strategy Canvases were first described by W Chan Kim and Renée Mauborgne in the mid 1990s. The Value Innovation Process has evolved the Strategy Canvas into a Value Curve with Metrics. In the strategy canvas the Elements of Performance:

- Are Listed on the bottom at a 45° angle as opposed to the left hand side.
- Are not rank ordered
- Do not have metrics

Value Curves are actionable with the addition of rank ordering and metrics.

Generating a Value Curve with Metrics:

There are three ways to create a list of Elements of Performance:

1. Put yourself in your Most Important Customer's shoes and ask, "What would be important to me?"

2. Use the Buyer Experience Cycle and The Seven Utility Levers (1, pages 122-125)

3. A Combination of 2 and 1.

We prefer the approach described in #1. It is used to develop the following Value Curve for a RE/MAX International Sales Affiliate. You will recall we reviewed the RE/MAX International Value Chain in Chapter 3.

You can do this individually, or, have the project team work together.

Suppose you are a sales affiliate helping your customers buy and sell residential and/or commercial real estate. What would be important to you? We suspect the first question would be: How much will I earn? Working in a RE/MAX franchisee office you would be paying a monthly fee. What is the fee/month? The franchisee and RE/MAX provide a number of services, that include standard items like an office, desk, phone, computer, internet connection, email address, business cards, etc. There are other critical issues that need to be answered. What constitutes advertising support? How are leads supplied? Are there qualified leads from RE/MAX? You perceive that the sales associates at RE/MAX have more experience than their competitors. They could be a good source of information. Another question: Where can I go for advice? Could I go to my peers? Listings are important in the world of real estate. Will my listings appear on the MLS?

These questions translate into Elements of Performance. Let's reflect on the questions you asked:

- How much will I earn?
- How much will it cost me/month?
- What advertising support will I get?
- How do I get leads?
- Will l get qualified leads from RE/MAX?
- Who gives advice?
- Are my listings on MLS?

Let's add to our list:

- What costs do I have to cover (health insurance, car expenses)?
- What costs will RE/MAX cover?
- What support materials are available?

The following table takes the questions and converts them into Elements of Performance.

Question	Element of Performance
How much will I earn?	Commission
How much will it cost me/month?	Operating Cost ($/mo.), Fixed Monthly Fee
What advertising support will I get?	Advertizing
How do I get leads?	Lead Generation, Qualified Leads
Will l get qualified leads from RE/MAX?	Qualified Leads
Where can I get advice?	Peer Experience, Franchise Support
Who will have access to my listings?	Listing Access, Global Reach
What costs do I have to cover (health insurance, car expenses.)	Benefits
What costs will RE/MAX cover?	Reimbursable Expenses
What support materials are available	Supportl Materials, Advertizing, Brand

Next, we finalize the list of Elements and rank order them. There are three ways we can rank order the Elements: Pairwise

Comparison (4), The Analytical Hierarchy Process (5) and User Rank.

Rank Ordering Tool	Ease of Use	Time to Complete
User Rank	Easiest	5 -10 minutes
Pairwise Comparison	Easier	15-20 minutes
Analytical Hierarchy Process	Hardest	2-3 hours

1. User Rank

This is the least sophisticated of the three methods but it is also the fastest. If you have a team of 4 for 5 people, a great way to rank order 12 Elements of Performance would be to list them on a flip chart, give each person five "hot dots" and have them put a "hot dot" next to their "Top 5 Elements." This is referred to as the Delphi approach.

2. Pairwise Comparison (PWC)

Pairwise Comparison refers to any process of comparing Elements of Performance in pairs to judge which of each Element is preferred by the Most Important Customer (4). e.g., If we took two Elements of Performance (Purchase Price and Disposal Cost) from the Police Car Value Curve, the Sheriff's Department would be required to identify which is more important, Purchase Price or Disposal Cost. We would expect they would say Purchase Price is more important than Disposal Cost. To Rank Order the Elements, every Element pair would be compared this way, one pair at a time. Our Slalom software provides this capability.

If you want to Rank Order Elements quickly, i.e., <15 minutes, we recommend you use the Pairwise Comparison approach.

3. Analytical Hierarchy Process (AHP)

The Analytical Hierarchy Process is a structured technique for organizing and analyzing complex decisions. Based on mathematics and psychology, it was developed by Thomas L. Saaty in the 1970's (5) and has been extensively studied and refined since then.

It is a more rigorous and refined process than Pairwise Comparison but it takes much longer to do than Pairwise Comparison. If you were to rank order ten Elements with a group of four or five people, the process could take 2 to 3 hours.

Here is an example of the Analytical Hierarchy Process for the Police Car example. In Figure 21, we see the dialog box which is presented when you use Slalom. It has called up a pair of Elements of Performance, Purchase Price and Disposal Cost and provides you with nine options to describe the relative importance between the two Elements.

Figure 21: Ranking of Elements of Performance using AHP

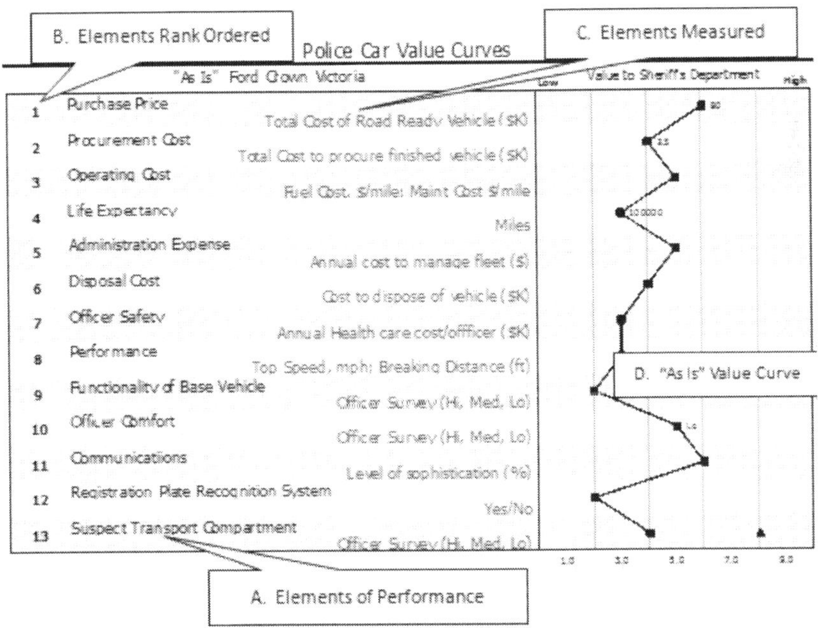

We are comparing the Elements, Purchase Price and Disposal Cost. Slalom software provides the individual or group doing the ranking with nine options. To advance to the next pair of Elements, click on the radial button opposite your preferred choice and the software will pull up the next pair for you to rank order.

When you have finished comparing all Elements, the software calculates how consistent you have been. If, for example, you said Purchase Price is more important than Disposal Cost and Disposal Cost is more important than Operator Safety and then selected Officer Safety is more important than Purchase Price, you would have been inconsistent. A consistency ratio of 20% or less is very good. Slalom automatically calculates this for you.

Here are the results of rank ordering the Elements for the RE/MAX International sales associate:

Element of Performance	Rank Order (Using AHP)
Commission	39
Peer Experience	19
Listing Access	13
Franchise Support	12
Fixed Monthly Fee	9
Advertising Support	6
Brand	6
Global Reach	4

The final step in developing the "As Is" Value Curve is to estimate the value being delivered by RE/MAX to the Sales Associate on a 1 to 9 scale (1 = Lo Value; 9 = Exceptional (Value) for each Element of Performance.

Element of Performance	Rank Order	Value Delivered
Commission	39	8.5
Peer Experience	19	8
Listing Access	13	8.5
Franchise Support	12	8
Fixed Monthly Fee	9	5
Advertising Support	6	7.5
Brand	6	7.5
Global Reach	4	7.5

We can now construct the Value Curve for the RE/MAX Sales Associate (See Figure 22):

Figure 22: Value Curve for a RE/MAX International Sales Associate

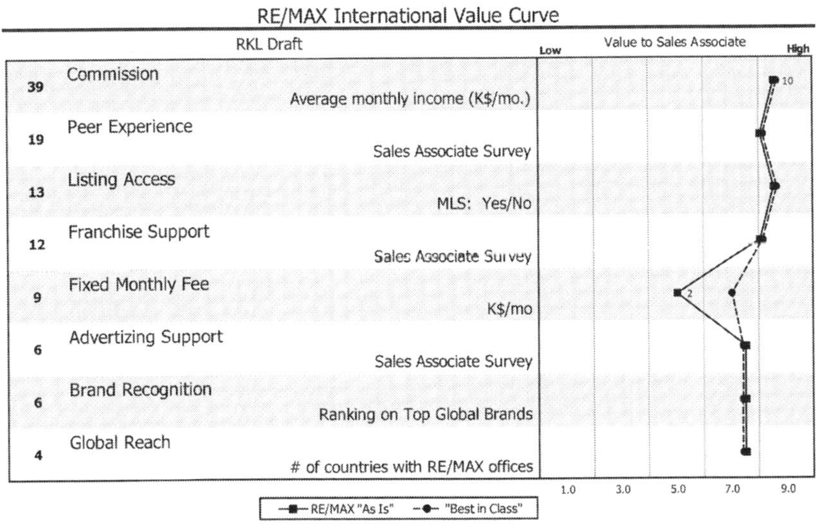

RE/MAX International is "Best in Class" for seven of the eight Elements of Performance. That is why the "As Is" and "Best in Class" curves overlap on all Elements except Fixed Monthly Fee. Associates working for Century21 and Prudential do not pay a monthly fee.

What does "Best in Class" mean? Assume we were putting together a Value Curve for a Ford Fusion. We may want to compare how it performs against the Hyundai Sonata, Honda Accord and the Toyota Camry. "Best in Class" would be the car that delivers the highest value on that Element of Performance, which could be the Ford Fusion. The car defined by the "Best in Class" curve may not exist. However, if you were able to put together a car with the combined best performance, the "Best In Class" Curve would define that car.

Value Curve Examples:

The best way to learn about Value Curves is to look at many examples and reflect on them. We will share six case studies with you to start your learning experience. As we did with Value Chains, we start with the least complex and build from there.

	Business	Business Type
1	"Pay as you Go" cell phones ➢ Virgin Mobile	B2C
2	Medical Device Manufacturers ➢ Knee Replacements in India ➢ Johnson and Johnson, Smith and Nephew and Stryker	B2B and B2C
3	Airports ➢ The International Traveler ➢ Hong Kong, Changi and others	B2B and B2C
4	LCD TVs (Consumer Electronic Products) ➢ Samsung, Sony and Sharp	B2C

5	Environmentally friendly packaging materials ➢ FoldedPak – ExpandOS	B2B, B2C and B2G
6	Fast Moving Consumer Packaged Goods (Branded products and Private Label) ➢ Novamin (Oravive toothpaste) ➢ Gsk, Sensodyne "Repair and Protect"	B2B and B2C

Is there just one Value Curve with Metrics for the Most Important Customer? Generally the answer is "Yes." One circumstance when this is not the case is Ms Consumer when she is presented with a purchase decision on a Fast Moving Consumer Packaged Good. You will see clearly when we present the Novamin case. There are three Value Curves with Metrics.

1. Virgin Group – Virgin Mobile

In 1999 Sir Richard Branson, invested £300 million of his own money, to fund Virgin Mobile. The global telecommunications industry was in meltdown. Virgin Group's partner in this joint venture was Deutsche Telecom.

<table>
<tr><td colspan="2">Virgin mobile</td></tr>
<tr><td>Business Type: B2C</td><td>Company: Virgin Group</td></tr>
<tr><td>Business: Pay as you go cell phone service</td><td>Most Important Customer: Parents, especially single mothers, with children</td></tr>
<tr><td colspan="2">Description: "Pay as you Go" was developed to provide additional safety to children. They could call their parents at any time. Minutes were purchased & downloaded to the phone - children could not generate huge phone bills.</td></tr>
</table>

Figure 23 compares "Pay as You Go" to regular cell phone service. The first three Elements of Performance show no difference in the value delivered to the parent in the two cell phone offerings. Where "Pay as you Go" wins out is on Operating Cost, Contract Length (there is no contract with "Pay as you Go") and Penalty for early cancellation (there is no contract to cancel with "Pay as you Go"). We do not know if Sir Richard used a Value Curve, but it was an innovation and other companies have since copied the Virgin Mobile model (e.g., AT&T, T Mobile in the US).

Figure 23: "Pay as You Go" Cell Phone Service Value Curve

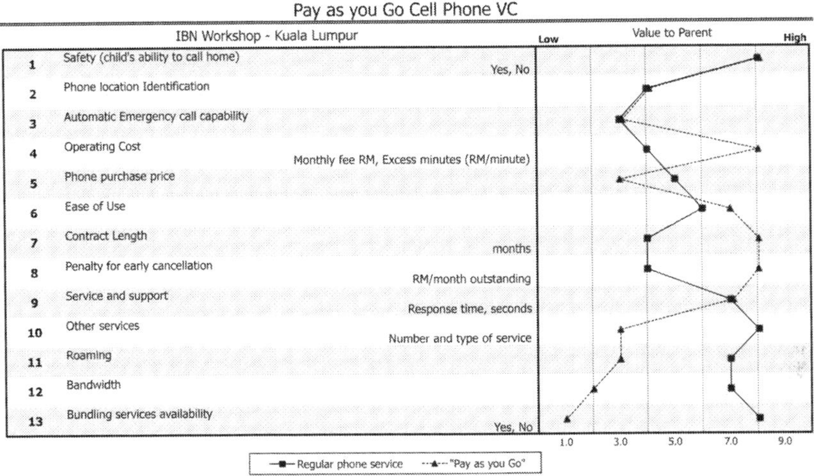

In the UK, Virgin Mobile was a smash hit. After four years of operation in Europe, Virgin Mobile had:

- 4 million customers
- Net Sales of £442MM
- EBITDA of £75MM

The business was sold July 4, 2006 for £1B to NTL Telewest. Telewest licensed the rights to use the Virgin name for £8.5MM/y and in February 2007, renamed the business Virgin Media.

2. Medical Device Manufacturers in India – providing knee replacements (Johnson and Johnson, Smith and Nephew and Stryker).

Recall the occurrence of osteoarthritis in India we described in Chapter 3? In India, with its large population, this is a huge challenge but a significant opportunity if you can deliver exceptional value to the Most Important Customer.

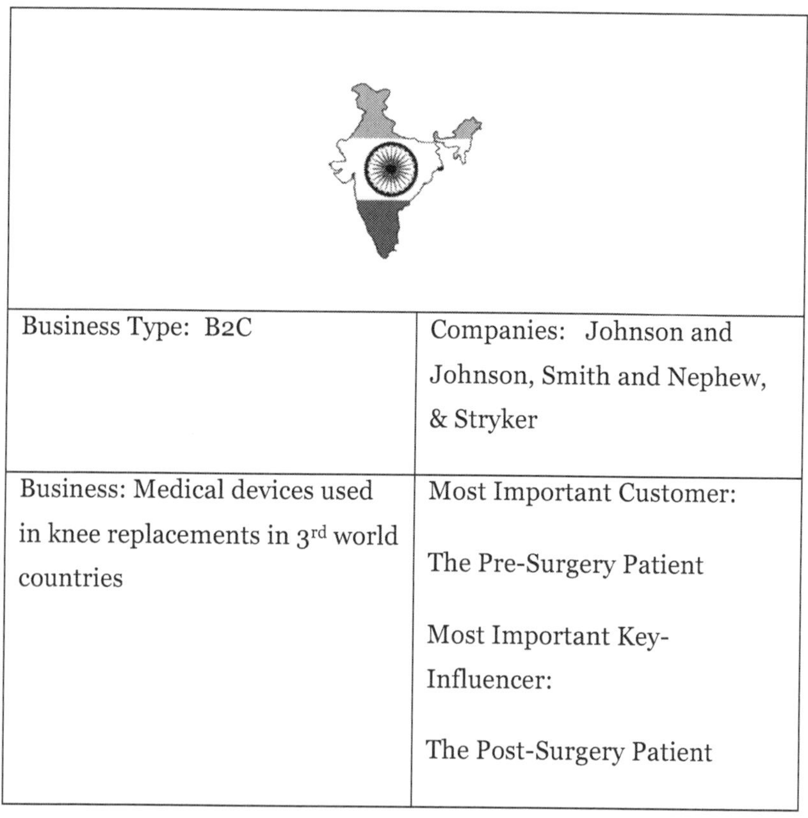

Business Type: B2C	Companies: Johnson and Johnson, Smith and Nephew, & Stryker
Business: Medical devices used in knee replacements in 3rd world countries	Most Important Customer: The Pre-Surgery Patient Most Important Key-Influencer: The Post-Surgery Patient

The Most Important Customer for a knee replacement is the osteo-arthritic Pre-Surgery Patient. If you are a manufacturer of replacement knees in India you need to develop and understand the Value Curve with Metrics for that Pre-Surgery Patient.

Figure 24: Value Curve with Metrics for a candidate for knee replacement in India

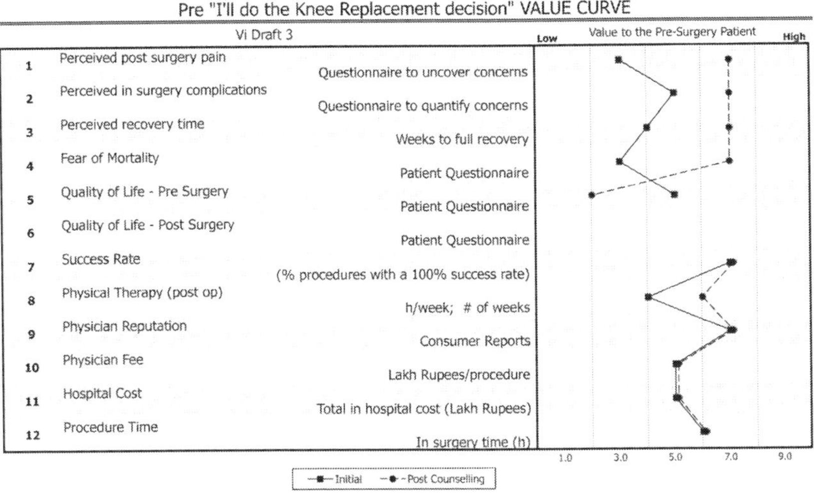

From this Value Curve, it is clear that the manufacturer needs to enlist a group of Post-Surgery patients who can help the pre-surgery patients understand that the risks are not as grave as they perceive. Most of the Indian population living in villages, some 600 million, have never been inside a hospital and have obvious fear. With the help of the existing network of free clinics who work through the cell phone network, there can be a bright future to solve this need.

3. The International Traveler – The world's airports

The international traveler is an airport's Most Important Customer. Travelers fund the airport's operations – next time take a look at your ticket and see how much you pay in airport taxes and landing fees. Are the Most Important Customer's needs being met? What changes could be made to improve conditions? An international airport is a city with many moving parts.

If there were recognition by all organizations: Government Agencies (Air Trafffic Control, Immigration, Customs, Security, Police, Fire Department, Medical Emergency, Transportation, etc.) and businesses (airlines, architects, engineering and planning, freight companies, general services, interior designers, maintenance, restaurants, space planners, surface transportation, etc.) that there is one Value Curve with Metrics that they should all be focused on, The Most Important Customer's needs could be met.

<table>
<tr><td colspan="2">香港國際機場 HONG KONG INTERNATIONAL AIRPORT</td></tr>
<tr><td>Business Type: B2C</td><td>Company: International Airports</td></tr>
<tr><td>Business: Handling hundreds of incoming and outgoing flights/day, managing aircraft surface movements, providing services to, and processing millions of passengers a year</td><td>Most Important Customer: The International Traveler</td></tr>
<tr><td colspan="2">Customers: International travelers from around the world; Airlines, Freight Companies; Retail; Restaurants; Surface transportation; Hotels, and more</td></tr>
</table>

Here's the Value Curve for the International Traveler.

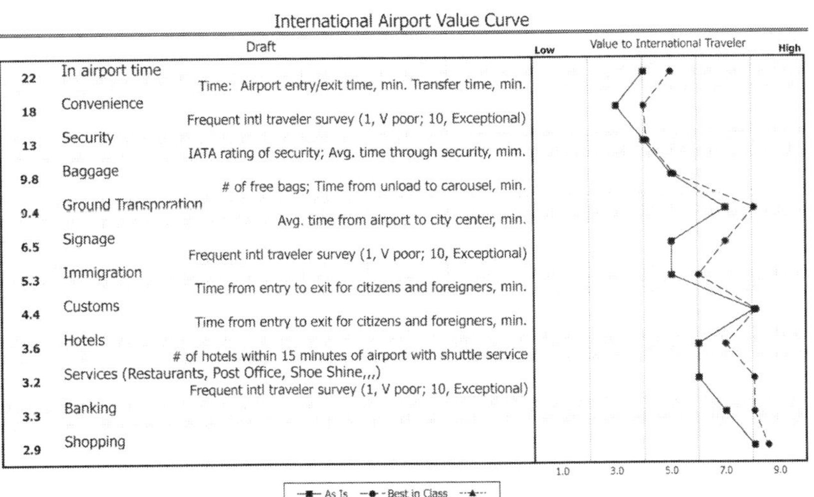

It should be the primary planning document for all stakeholders involved in the design, construction, and operation of an international airport. All stakeholders should collaborate in all aspects, e.g., passengers do not need to be checked on three separate occasions: Security, Immigration and Customs. This could be handled with one retinal scan. All international travelers with validated passports and a retinal scan on file could be handled on an exception basis.

The value being delivered to the Most Important Customer on Elements of major importance is lower than the value being delivered on Elements of low importance to the Most Important Customer. This is backwards.

4. Samsung Electronics – LCD TVs in the US Market

Samsung has vaulted from being the doormat of the Consumer Electronics Industry to vying with Apple to be the Rule Maker.

In 2005, the Business Unit responsible for the marketing, manufacturing and sales was very concerned about their US market share for LCD TVs. They formed a dedicated project team, located the team in the Value Innovation Process Center in Suwon and charged them with selling 1 million more units a year in the US.

SAMSUNG	
Business Type: B2C	Company: Samsung Electronics
Business: Consumer Electronics - LCD TVs	Most Important Customer: The US Consumer
Goal: Sell 1 million more units in the US	

After interviewing consumers in the US, the team developed a Value Curve (See Figure 25). We have not seen it but based on the articles written in Business Week (6), we believe the following Value Curve is a good facsimile.

Figure 25: "As Is" Value Curve for LCD TVs in the US (2005)

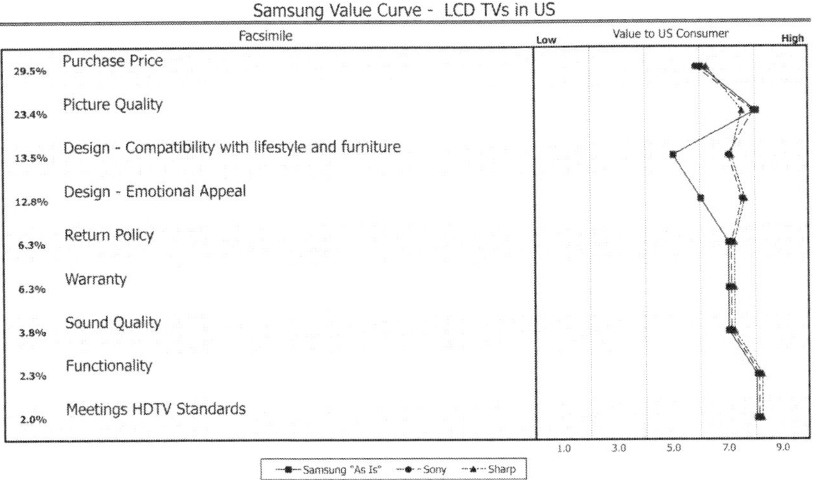

The team concluded their LCD TVs were delivering:

1. Essentially the same value to the US Consumer on the following Elements of Performance: Price, Picture Quality, Return Policy, Warranty, etc. as Sharp and Sony.

2. Lower value than Sony and Sharp on both Elements of Performance dealing with design.

They were swimming in a red ocean with their LCD TV offering in the US. When you see Value Curves overlapping like this, you are swimming in a red ocean.

You will notice that the Elements of Performance have been rank ordered differently than previous Value Curves. In this case, we have used the Analytical Hierarchy Process. We can see the relative difference in importance between the Elements. The Top 4 Elements account for 80% of the 100 points that are available, i.e, the team needs to focus on Price, Picture Quality and Design (See Figure 26) . The other Elements of Performance have little importance to the US consumer.

Figure 26: Samsung "To Be" Value Curve with Metrics for LCD TVs in the US

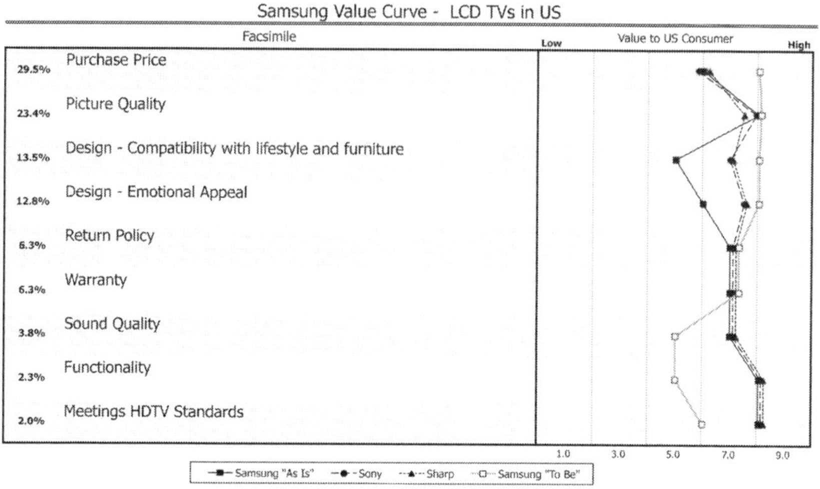

Samsung Value Curve - LCD TVs in US

Facsimile — Value to US Consumer (Low – High)

Weight	Attribute
29.5%	Purchase Price
23.4%	Picture Quality
13.5%	Design - Compatibility with lifestyle and furniture
12.8%	Design - Emotional Appeal
6.3%	Return Policy
6.3%	Warranty
3.8%	Sound Quality
2.3%	Functionality
2.0%	Meetings HDTV Standards

1.0 3.0 5.0 7.0 9.0

Samsung "As Is" — Sony — Sharp — Samsung "To Be"

5. FoldedPak - ExpandOS™

FoldedPak was formed in 2003 with venture capital funding. ExpandOS is a packing material cut from recycled cardboard and folded into a pyramid (See Figure 27). It is far more environmentally friendly than bubble wrap, chips or peanuts. The company initially focused on the industrial market focusing on the pack out station at the end of a production line (See Figure 28). This model had several drawbacks: Low utilization rates (<10%) and high capital investment (K$10/machine). In addition the machines were not very reliable (around 50%). In 2009, FoldedPak used the Value Innovation Process to determine what they should do to turn the company around. Details on the FoldedPak and ExpandOS are provided in the figures below. The investors brought in Duart Capital to determine if FoldedPak could be saved. They used the Value Innovation Process and developed the "As Is" Value Curve for a manufacturer who used machines at the pack out station (See Figure 29), It shows that Expandos reduced damage in the shipping process. However, Total Cost, Ease of Use, Product Cost and Acceptance, Expandos was delivering less value than Peanuts.The "As Is" Value Curve became the starting point for the reinvention of FoldedPak and ExpandOS.

Table 3: Background on FoldedPak – Expandos.

ExpandOS	
Business Type: B2B, B2C and B2G	Company: FoldedPak
Business: New packaging material - ExpandOS™	Most Important Customer: Manufacturers, Overnight Shippers, Mass Merchants and Postal Services
Example: ExpandOS was developed to reduce bubble wrap. Peanuts and chips in packaging fragile products.	
Customers: Canada Post, CoorsTek, Home Depot, hp, Public Storage, Staples, UPS	

Figure 27: ExpandOS was invented in 2003. Once the package is sealed, the serrated edges lock the pyramids in place so contents in the package do not move in transit. (The pyramid has a 3.2cm x 3.2cm Base and stands 3.5cm high) 	**Figure 28: The original machine was installed at the pack out station at the end of a production line.** They were used about 10% of the time and machine reliability was poor. 

Figure 29: "As Is" Value Curve for ExpandOS

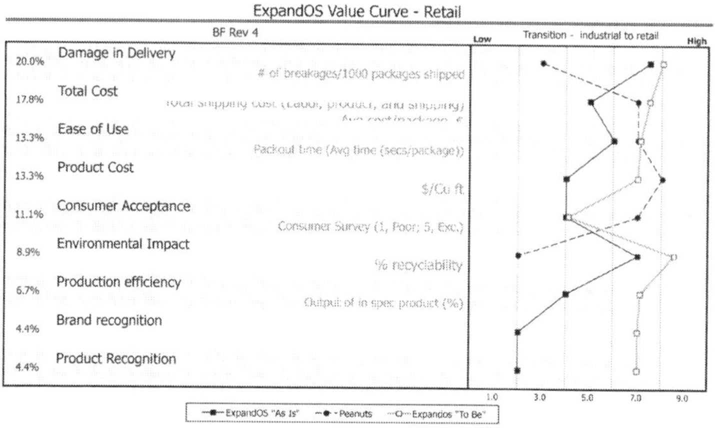

ExpandOS Value Curve - Retail

BF Rev 4

Low Transition - industrial to retail High

20.0% Damage in Delivery
# of breakages/1000 packages shipped

17.8% Total Cost
Total shipping cost (Labor, product, and shipping)

13.3% Ease of Use
Packout time (Avg time (secs/package))

13.3% Product Cost
$/Cu ft

11.1% Consumer Acceptance
Consumer Survey (1, Poor; 5, Exc.)

8.9% Environmental Impact
% recyclability

6.7% Production efficiency
Output of in spec product (%)

4.4% Brand recognition

4.4% Product Recognition

1.0 3.0 5.0 7.0 9.0

ExpandOS "As Is" — Peanuts — Expandos "To Be"

We will come back to ExPandOS in Chapter 6 when we look at "To Be" Value Curves with Metricsand share more about turning this company around. It is a great case study!

6. Novamin – Oravive Toothpaste (Now the primary active ingredient in GlaxoSmithKline's Sensodyne Repair and Protect toothpaste)

Novamin is a technology company that was spun out of US Biomaterials in 2003 and acquired by GlaxoSmithKline in 2009.

- Late 1960s: University of Florida Professor Larry Hench developed bioactive glass as a bone replacement material.
- Mid-1990s: US Biomaterials Corp. licensed bioactive glass. Len Litkowski, a dentist on the faculty at the University of Maryland, believed that Novamin (a bioactive glass) could be used to regenerate teeth.
- October 2003: the first product with NovaMin was launched - SootheRx prescription toothpaste by 3M/Omni.
- April 2004: Novamin received its first round of $10 million venture capital funding from Intersouth Partners

of Durham, N.C. Later that year, Novamin received its first over-the-counter clearance from the US FDA.

- 2005: Novamin, the company, made Oravive toothpaste available for purchase over the internet. It had a 5% loading of Novamin in it but no NaF.
- 2007: The first consumer toothpastes were launched in three European brands. They contained the Novamin active ingredient but not fluoride.
- 2008: Novamin received a second round of $2.5 million venture capital from Harbert Venture Partners of Birmingham, AL.
- December, 2008: Nupro with NovaMin, a cleaner for dental hygienists, was launched by Dentsply International.
- December, 2009: GSK acquired Novamin for $135 million (a 980% ROI for the investors)
- May, 2010: Smith Kline Beecham, a unit of GSK, launches Sensodyne Repair and Protect toothpaste in Europe, selling a 75ml tube for £4.

Here's a close-up of the effect of Novamin, the bioactive glass, on the tooth:

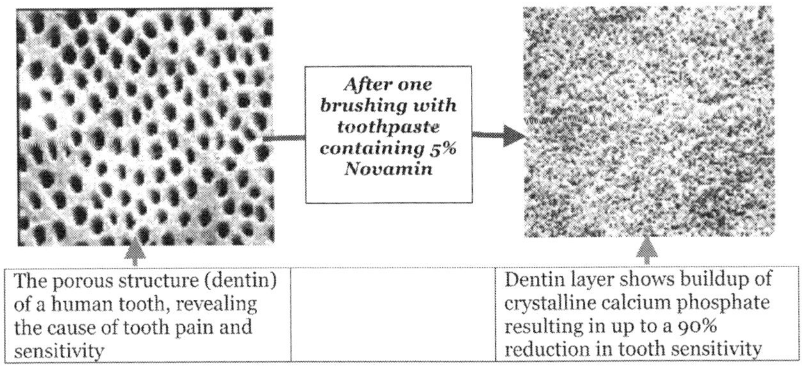

Novamin was a technology company that had a molecule (bioactive glass with the same name as the company) that could repair teeth but it faced tough, very expensive choices. What to do?

1. Make the investment in the clinical trials to demonstrate the efficacy of a fluoride Novamin combination in different toothpaste formulations.

2. Try to convince the global Fast Moving Consumer Packaged Goods companies who manufactured, marketed and sold toothpaste that Novamin would allow them to deliver exceptional value to their Most Important Customer and gain market share.

3. Make the investment to become a toothpaste manufacturer and market its limited product line and unknown brand to mass merchants, supermarkets, pharmacies, and chemists around the world and win the Zeroth and First Moments of Truth with consumers. This would be difficult, if not impossible.

In 2005, Value Innovations, Inc. worked with Novamin to develop a family of Value Curves with Metrics. We also developed and facilitated a Key Expert Panel (KEP) to help the company make the critical decisions and chart the course forward. There were retired, or ex members of, Church and Dwight, Colgate Palmolive, and Procter and Gamble attending. Unilever couldn't make their schedules work and I distinctly remember GSK was really not interested at that time. Len Litkowksi attended the KEP too.

<table>
<tr><td colspan="2">NovaMin
Technology, Inc.</td></tr>
<tr><td>Business Type: Was B2B; Now B2C</td><td>Company: Originally Novamin; Now GlaxoSmithKline (GSK purchased Novamin in May, 2009)</td></tr>
<tr><td>Business: FMCPG</td><td>Most Important Customer:

Originally the FMCPG Company;

Now the Consumer</td></tr>
<tr><td colspan="2">Description: Novamin is a patented material (sodium calcium phosphosilicate) that reacts with saliva and lays down a very thin layer of material to restore the dentin layer of the teeth</td></tr>
</table>

Novamin's Value Chain was short. As a manufacturer of Oravive, they were a true B2C company, selling product on line. Oravive, with a 5% loading of Novamin, did not have NaF as an additive.

At the same time they were in negotiations with all the major producers of toothpaste. The goal was to enter into an Agreement with at least one of the major producers to license their technology, or sell the company.

Here is Novamin's Value Chain:

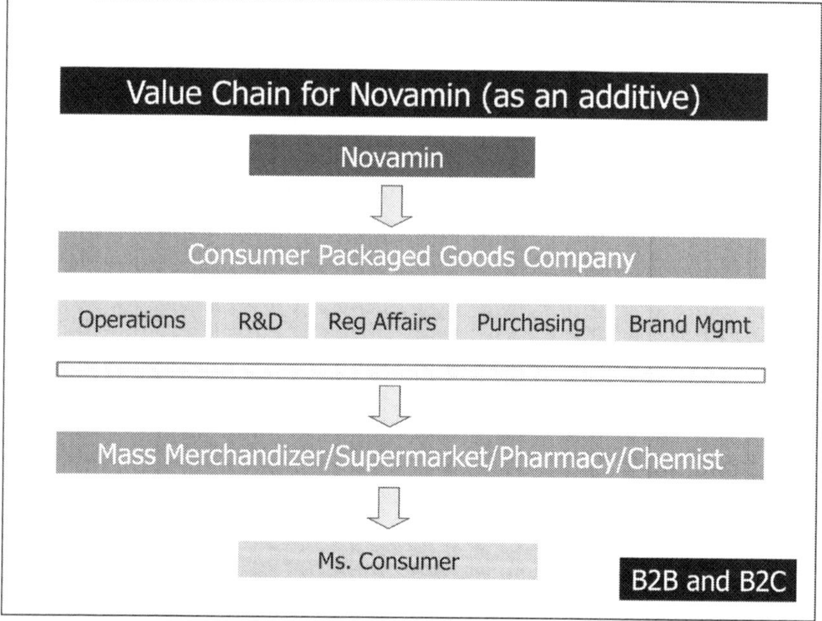

Understanding the Value Curves with Metrics were critical for Novamin to move forward to close a deal with a FMCPG company:

- The FMCPG company (The Most Important Customer within this company would change as the negotiations and product development advanced)
- The Mass Merchant
- Ms Consumer

Unknown to us in 2006 and adding another level of complexity, the Fast Moving Packaged Goods company needed to win the Zeroth, First and Second Moments of truth with Ms. Consumer

Moments of Truth and why it is important to understand them

The Value Curves for the three Moments of Truth are entirely different. Procter and Gamble has stated publicly they need to win 4.8 billion Moments of Truth a day. Many of us in the world of B2B think those companies working in the B2C world have it easy. They do not.

Moment of Truth	Definition
Zeroth (ZMOT)	The company has delivered consistent and meaningful value to Ms Consumer in the products she uses from the company, so she is willing to try a new product manufactured and marketed by that same company
First (FMOT)	Ms. Consumer determines she will buy the product based on what she sees and reads on the package. Feel of the package may play a role also (This is especially true for products like toilet paper and face tissue). Winning the First Moment of Truth with the first time buyer is the first step a FMCPG company takes in growing market share
Second (SMOT)	Ms. Consumer opens the product, uses it at home and is delighted by how the product performs

Value Curves with Metrics for the ZMOT, SMOT and FMOT are different. In the world of FMCPG you need to develop three Value Curves for your product whether it's a brand or a private label.

Winning the Zeroth and First Moments of truth would be especially important for the Fast Moving Packaged Goods with their new toothpaste containing Novamin. Packaging plays a major role in winning these two moments of truth. We were not at all surprised to see the Sensodyne Repair and Protect package. It is absolutely stunning (See Figure 30). Five Fresnel lenses (two circles of 2.5cm in diameter and three of 1.8 cm in diameter) in aquamarine and white explain how Repair and

Protect works. These 3D images really catch your eye when you are walking down the supermarket aisle. Even at £4 per 75ml tube, you have a real sense that Repair and Protect will win a lot of Zeroth and First Moments of Truth in Europe where the product is currently on sale. The product does reduce tooth sensitivity, so we would fully expect Repair and Protect will win close to 100% of the Second Moments of Truth.

Figure 30: Sensodyne Repair and Protect Toothpaste

(first toothpaste package in the world to use Fresnel lens technology - image is flat but looks 3-D)

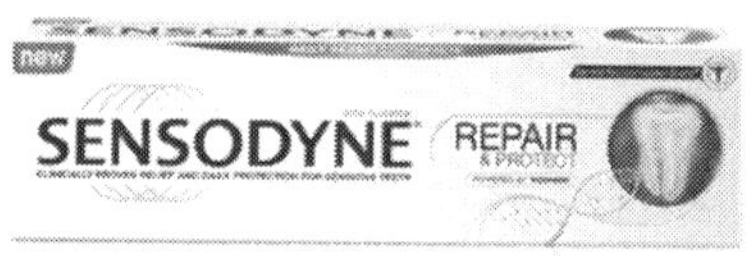

Repair and Protect is available in Europe. In the UK, it sells for £4 per 75ml tube. For more about GSK's Sensodyne Repair and Protect, the fastest selling new toothpaste in years, go to https://sensodyne.com.sg/.

Figure 31: Facsimile of the Value Curve with Metrics for a recognized brand name toothpaste with NovaminMost Important Customer: Ms. Consumer – Zeroth Moment of Truth

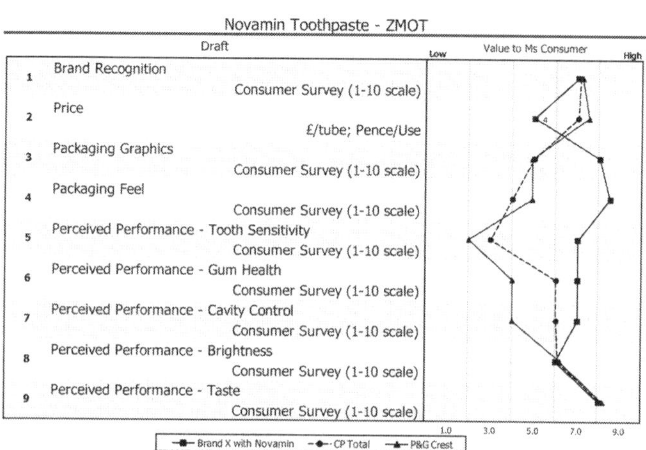

It was assumed the branded toothpaste with Novamin would be sold at a premium price (lower value delivered to Ms Consumer) but she would justify paying the premium because of better perceived performance (higher value delivered) on Tooth Sensitivity; Gum Health; Cavity Control; Brightness and Taste. This Value Curve (See Figure 31) shows Brand Recognition for GSK's Sensodyne Repair and Protect, Colgate Palmolive's Total and P&G's Oral B are essentially the same. If Novamin were selling the toothpaste as opposed to GSK, the value delivered on brand recognition would very low (perhaps 1 or 2), i.e., Novamin's success rates at winning the ZMOT and FMOT would be very low.

There are three factors in play at the time of writing this book: The Sensodyne brand is well recognized and associated with reducing tooth pain. The package is stunning and GSK is aggressively advertizing Repair and Protect at least in the UK. They are winning the ZMOT and FMOT and, Ms Consumer is paying the premium price.

Let's compare the ZMOT Value Curve for Ms Consumer with the one for the Department Merchandiser in the Mass Merchant company (See Figure 32).

Figure 32: Facsimile of Value Curve with Metrics for the Department Merchandiser at the Mass Merchant, Supermarket, Pharmacy or Chemist

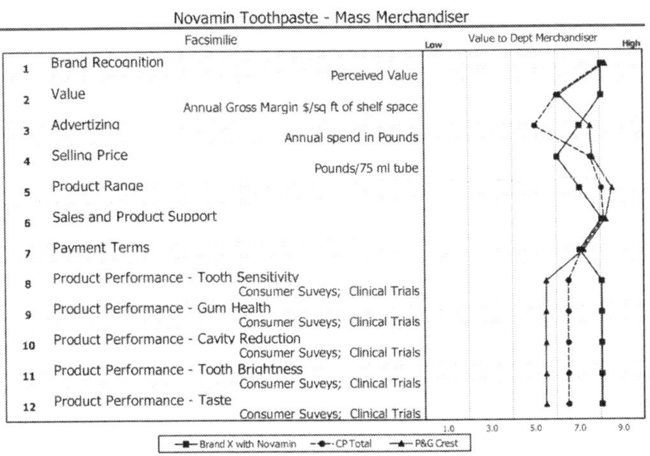

Brand recognition is the most important Element of Performance in both Value Curves. With that exception, theValue Curves are dramatically different. For the Department Merchandiser, Value (The gross profit per unit area of shelf space), and advertizing investment the Fast Moving Packaged Goods company plans to promote and support the product, are the second and third most important Elements. The Department Merchandiser probably sees Brand Recognition for GSK, Colgate Palmolive and Procter and Gamble about the same. Colgate Palmolive typically spends less on advertizing (lower value) than P&G. Most importantly, the Department Merchandiser sees the opportunity to increase his/her gross margin $ or £ or €/ unit area of shelf space with this new product. In reality in the UK, it looks as though GSK is investing more in advertizing than the competition and with Repair and Protect successfully selling £4 per tube, the gross margin contribution per unit shelf area has to be very attractive for all the major mass merchants, supermarkets, pharmacies and chemists in Europe. Figure 33 provides a comparison of some toothpaste prices for the three brands, Colgate Palmolive, P&G's Oral B and GSK's Sensodyne at Tesco in the UK:

Figure 33: Prices of toothpaste at Tesco

Manufacturer	Product	Size (ml)	Price (£/unit)	Price (£/75 ml)
Colgate	Total	100	2.29	1.72
	Sensitive Pro Relief	75	3.56	3.56
	Advanced White Toothpaste	100	1.10	0.83
Oral B	Pro expert Enamel Shield	75	1.75	1.75
	Pro Expert Sensitive	100	1.75	1.31
	Complete Extra White	100	2.49	1.87
GSK	Sensodyne Repair and Protect	75	4.00	4.00

Downloaded from Tesco's website, February 6, 2012

The only toothpaste coming close to Repair and Protect in price is Colgate Palmolive's Sensitive Pro Relief, at £3.56/75ml tube. Compared to Colgate's and Oral B regular toothpaste offerings, Sensodyne is selling successfully at a huge premium.

Let's take a look at the Value Curve for the Brand Manager within the FMCPG company (See Figure 34).

Figure 34: Facsimile of Value Curve with Metrics for the Brand Manager at the FMCPG Company

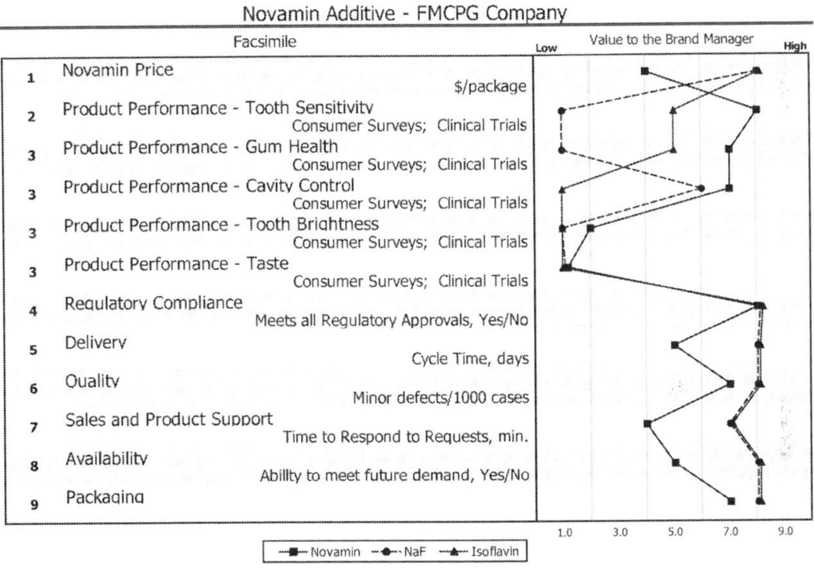

It is easy to see why a Brand Manager at a Fast Moving Consumer Packaged Goods company would be reluctant to support moving forward with Novamin back in 2005:

- It was high priced
- Market research needed to be carried out with consumers to confirm the results of the clinical trials
- R&D and manufacturing had to assure that Novamin was compatible with their existing toothpaste/manufacturing processes

Next Steps:

1. Work with your pilot projects to develop "As Is" and "Best in Class" Value Curves with Metrics for the Most Important Customers:
    - ➢ Assemble your teams
    - ➢ Have them develop a list of Elements of Performance
    - ➢ Each team chose the rank ordering tool they want to use
    - ➢ Rank order the Elements
    - ➢ Define metrics for each Element
    - ➢ If you have absolute numbers for the metrics, capture them and use them as the team generates Value Curves with Metrics using Slalom
    - ➢ Select the scale you want to use for your value curves (we recommend 1-9)
    - ➢ Estimate the value being delivered for the Elements for the "As Is" and "Best in Class" cases
    - ➢ Use Slalom to generate Value Curves with Metrics
2. Have the teams meet, share their Value Curves with Metrics, critique same and revise where necessary

You are now ready to move to Step 4 of the Value Innovation Process.

Takeaways:

1. "As Is" and "Best in Class" Value Curves with Metrics provide a clear picture on the value being delivered to your Most Important Customers for your product or service today.
2. An Element of Performance is a capability or characteristic of your product, service or offering that is important to the Most Important Customer and can be performed/observed in a measurable way.
3. An Element of Performance is succinct. It is not an objective nor a feature.
4. Elements of Performance must be measured and rank ordered.
5. There are three ways to develop Elements of Performance:
    - ➢ Put yourself in your Most Important Customer's shoes
    - ➢ The 7x7 Matrix
    - ➢ A combination of both

6. You have three ways to rank order Elements of Performance:
    - User Rank (Easiest to do, takes 5-10 minutes)
    - Pairwise Comparison (Easy to do, takes 15-20 minutes)
    - Analytical Hierarchy Process (Tougher to do, takes 2-3h)
7. Fast Moving Consumer Packaged Goods companies, for both branded and private label products, need to develop Value Curves with Metrics for the Zeroth, First and Second Moments of Truth.
8. Venture capital and equity investors can increase their investment success rates using the Value Innovation Process.
9. You can use Value Curves and Metrics to guide your decisions whether you are a B2B, B2C, B2G or a Not-For-Profit.
10. Technology companies (e.g., Novamin) can significantly benefit using these tools.
11. Not-For-Profits need to develop Value Curves with Metrics for their Most Important
12. Customers on the sponsor and delivery sides of their business.

CHAPTER 5

"If I had asked what they need, they would have said faster horses."

Henry Ford, date and place unknown

Value Innovation Process Step #4:

Contextual Interviews: Uncovering the Most Important Customer's unmet needs

The Value Innovation Process turns on how well this step is performed. All of the information that has been gathered in the first 3 steps comes into play in this crucial step. Every element within this step must be carried out precisely to achieve the desired result. It is very exciting to see your work culminate here and in the following steps.

Contextual Interviews in the Value Innovation Process

Three interviews – Nominally 1h in length

Step	Focus	Objectives
4	Divergent, Listening	Uncover the Most Important Customers' challenges & unmet needs
6-7	Convergent, Shaping	Critique "As Is" & "To Be" Value Curves with Metrics
10	Convergent, Defining	Finalize Value Curve. Review "How" to deliver the "What"

Clay Christensen and Martin Raynor shared traditional market research may be able to tell you: The size of the market. Who the players are. How fast the market is growing. How the product is priced. The competitors and their strengths and weaknesses. That has not told you anything about what it is you must do to meet unmet customer needs. You must understand the jobs your product/service was hired to do – the problems they need to solve (1).

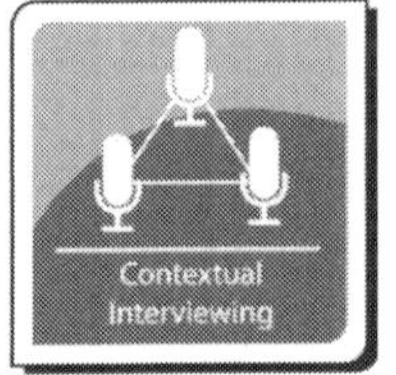	**What is Contextual Interviewing?:** A process to uncover the unmet, unarticulated needs of your Most Important Customers. There are three interviews, each 1h in length, carried out at different times with an interview team and 2 Most Important Customers. The interviews each have a different focus: Divergent (Listening); Convergent (Shaping) and Convergent (Defining)

	**Who is your Most Important Customer?:** You defined your Most Important Customer by developing a Value Chain and used the 3 Questions and the Three Question Template (Refer back to Chapter 3).

Setting up the capability: Our preferred setup and format for a Contextual Interview is shown in Figure 35. This is not recommended for use by Fast Moving Consumer Package Goods companies observing Ms Consumer but would be recommended for Fast Moving Consumer Package Goods companies when interviewing department merchandisers.

Figure 35: Recommended details for Contextual Interviews

1	Interview Team	
	Cross functional	4-5 members
	Lead Interviewer	One person selected on the basis of ISPI or KAI scores/indexes
	Scribes	1 or 2
	Colocated	No
2	Format	Telecon
	Preferred Provider	ReadyTalk
	Recorded	Yes
3	Interviewees	2
	Colocated	Not required
4	# of Interviews (1st, 2nd and 3rd Rounds)	3
	Number of interviews/round	6
	Interview length	1h
5	Interview Instrument Format	
	Introduction, Goals, Wrap Up	Developed by team
	# of questions	6 - 10
	# of days sent out ahead of time	2-3
6	Interview Output	
	Audio Recordings	Stored on company server
	Transcription of recordings by	Verbalink
	Transcribed Recordings	Stored on company server
	Access Rights	Need to be defined

The interview team and the interviewee pairs remain the same throughout the interview process. If an interviewee has to cancel, reschedule the interview. The lead interviewer must remain the same throughout.

To Be Effective:

The Team: The team is selected from the project team if one exists. A mix, as much as possible, of different functional areas:

- Business Development
- Corporate Growth
- Engineering
- Manufacturing/Distribution
- Marketing
- R&D

Contextual Interviewing, the fourth round of the Value Innovation Process is so important that it belongs to all functional areas of the company. The outputs from these three rounds of interviews could potentially change the face of, and direction of, your company.

Roles and Responsibilities: The team should determine who is responsible for the following:

- Instrument development
- Selection of interviewees
- Setting up pilots
- Scribe(s)
- Preparation of interview output (including transcription)
- Primary contact person for interviewee
- Communications central

Format: There are a number of options available.

- Observe live: There is much to be learned by watching your product or service in use. Watching the installation of software, international travelers as they move from the terminal entrance to boarding their flight, heavy equipment operators who are grading or mining, Ms Consumer shopping, etc. But we want to talk to Subject Matter Experts (Your Most Important Customer) and take advantage of their experience in many situations, not just one.

- Video recording
  - ✓ Attended by an anthropologist
  - ✓ Unattended using either a single, or multiple cameras

  This process was used by IDEO when they were asked to redesign the front entrance of a hospital (2)
- Face to Face meeting/interview: This is expensive. The process of flying interview team members and/or two interviewees to the location where the interview is being held actually reduces productivity because of travel. It can be threatening to the interviewees. It may also be difficult to co-locate two interviewees.
- Videoconference: This typically requires a videoconferencing center for the team and perhaps for the interviewees. At this point with technology, this is a limitation. Skype is always an option but there are many instances, particularly when people are working outdoors, e.g. commercial and residential repaint contractors, heavy equipment operators, truck drivers, police officers, project managers for large construction projects, where computer access is not possible.
- Teleconference: This is the least expensive, least intrusive option. The interview team can be in different locations and the two interviewees can also be in different locations. Most people have telephone access. Even in India, where half the population has a daily family income of <70INR, the villagers have a mobile phone or access to one.

Interviewees: In our experience the ideal number of interviewees is 2. With just one interviewee, the spotlight and pressure is always on that person. With two people:

1. The pressure is not always on one person.

2. The second interviewee has time to think and reflect on what the other interviewee has shared.

Rather than being an interview, it becomes a discussion. A comment made by one interviewee can broaden the discussion. We find about 1/3 of the time interviewees share at the end, they really enjoy the interaction. Three interviewees make it very difficult to get through the instrument in 1 hour.

People have raised the objection that with 2 interviewees, one influences the other, i.e., you are poisoning the well. While we certainly understand this objection, our experience is quite the opposite. The interview pairs are not connected in any way and yet the conversations bear a remarkable similarity. In our experience, when we compare the outputs from interview pairs from 6 separate interviews, we start to hear the same thing. From this experience, we cap the interviews at 6. Is 6 statistically significant? No. Will we learn anything new from additional interviews? Our experience is that this is highly unlikely.

Interview Leader: Tom Kelley has published two books, "The Art of Innovation" and "The Ten Faces of Innovation." (2, 3) Kelley describes 10 types of people in the world who have a role to play in innovation and identifies the anthropologist as the ideal person to lead contextual interviews. Why? Because the anthropologist is always asking questions. They are always asking "Why". How do you identify the lead interviewers? Using the KAI Index or ISPI.

Kirton Adaption-Innovation:

We recommend the lead interviewer have a KAI Index of >110. For more information on KAI, go to http://www.kaicentre.com/ok2.htm.

The Kirton Adaption-Innovation Inventory (KAI) contains 32 items and can be completed in 15-20 minutes. Each item is scored using a Leikert scale (1 to 5), so the lowest and highest possible scores are 32 and 160 with an average of 95. It was developed by Dr Michael J Kirton (4).

KAI is concerned with the different ways people think, and particularly the way they show their creativity, solve problems and make decisions. A simple description of Adaptors and Innovators (as two groups and not a continuum) is shown below in Figure 36. With a KAI Index increasingly >95 you are increasingly comfortable in unstructured environments and like a lack of policies and procedures. With a KAI Index of <95 you are increasingly comfortable in structured environments, policies and procedures in place etc.

Figure 36: KAI Adaptor – Innovator Profiles

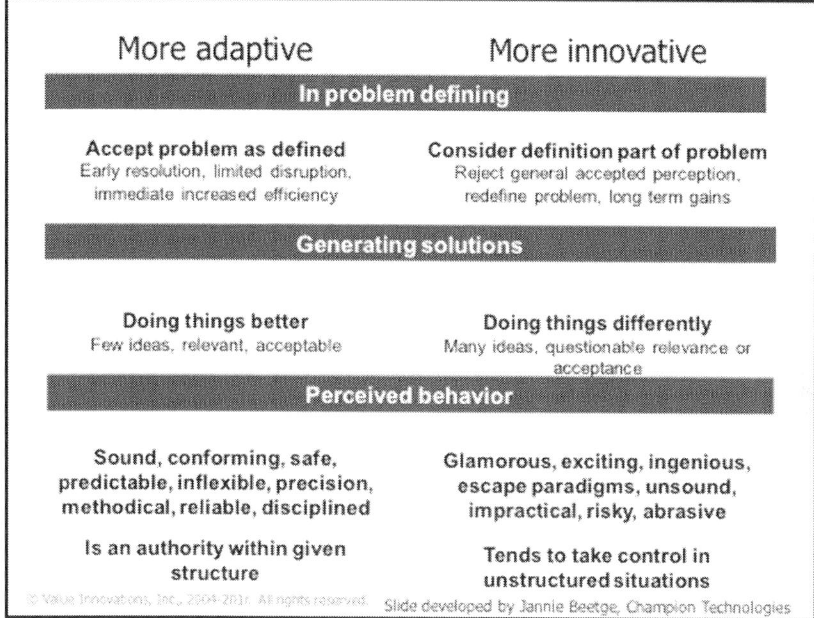

Innovation Strengths Preference Indicator

Bob Rosenfeld, CEO of Idea Connection Systems, is the creator of the tool ISPI (Innovation Strengths Preference Indicator). It highlights 12 orientations that compose an individual's predispositions for a certain type of innovation. It makes visible the way an individual prefers to solve problems and what impacts their motivation, passion and decision-making. The ISPI also shows how one prefers to work with others and deal with control (5). These orientations impact innovation results.

The ISPI is taken online at a dedicated secure website. It consists of 50 questions that take 15 to 20 minutes to complete. You can take the ISPI as an individual or create an organizational or team specific database. We see ISPI as a more sophisticated tool than KAI Index.

We do not to pretend to be experts in this area. We encourage you to dig deeper. What we know is, poor lead interviewers will kill you, just like average project leaders.

Developing the 1st Round Instrument: There are three major sections:

- **Background:**
  - Why this effort is being made
  - Why the interviewees have been selected
  - The objectives
  - Any special circumstances, such as: "You will be joined by another expert and the session will be recorded."
  - What is in it for those being interviewed (A gift card for $100; an honorarium, a leather jacket with a logo embossed on it, etc.)

- **6 to 10 open ended questions.** We recommend you select from the following lists:

  This is the question we always start with:
  - What are the issues keeping you awake at night (in your business)?

  Followed by:

  - What are the critical issues you will face over the next 3 to 5 years in your job?
  - What changes do you expect to see in the next 3 to 5 years?

At the outset, do not limit the discussion to your products and services . If you do you will not uncover new potential opportunities for your organization that are outside the scope of this project or even your company's current mission. Jeffrey Gitomer in his book, "The Little Green Book of Getting Your Way," (6) provides 18 power lead-ins which are very useful in crafting open ended questions for 1st Round interviews:

What has been your experience...	What have you found...
How have you successfully used...	What do you propose when...
What are you doing to ensure..	What do they do in this circumstance...
What makes you choose...	How do your customers react to...
What is the one thing you would improve about...	How might your customers react to...
What would you change about...	What are you doing to keep...
Are there other factors...	How are you currently....
What do you look for...	How often do you contact...
What is the determining or deciding factor when...	

We have provided you with 21 potential questions, so drafting 6 to 10 should be relatively easy. You will pilot the first interview. That will provide an opportunity to see how the questions flow and whether you need to add/modify, the questions.

Will the 6 to 10 questions be the only questions asked? No. The primary responsibility of the lead interviewer is to listen and ask follow up questions. The Elements of Performance you developed in the "As Is" Value Curve should be sitting in front of the lead interviewer. They can prompt any number of follow up questions. By the time the interview is completed, somewhere between 30 and 50 questions will have been asked.

- **Wrap Up.** This includes:
    - An evaluation of the value of the session to them (on a 1-5 scale (1 = Low Value; 5 = Exceptional Value)
    - What they've learned as a result of this interview
    - What they enjoyed most about the session
    - What they liked the least about the session
    - What we should do differently in future interviews
    - Win a commitment for a date and time for the next interview.

The Do's:

Set up an interview team	1h maximum length
Define roles and responsibilities	Interview 2 Most Important Customers at same time
Develop and pilot an instrument	Get consent and record the interviews
No more than 12 questions	Ask for feedback
Make it fun	Win commitment for 2 more interviews
Listen to new voices with new Ears – Interview new people within the Most Important Customer category	Be prepared to move away from the instrument
In the 1st and 2nd Round interviews, resist conclusions and discussions of solutions to problems. Capture them in a parking lot	

The Don'ts:

Do not ask "What do you need?" because:

- Interviewees don't know what they don't know

- Interviewees don't know what you could do

As soon as you ask, what do you need? ...... you are back to the world of incrementalism, the very thing Henry Ford wanted to avoid.

Here is the list of Don'ts we have developed after doing hundreds of these interviews.

Interview Purchasing Agents
Have one person doing this
Let the interview drag
Let the interview go over 1h
No pauses
Use more than 12 written questions
Don't show interviewees a Value Curve

Preparing for the 1st round interviews:

Identifying and recruiting the Most Important Customers: We identified the Most Important Customer (as a group) in Step 2 of the Value Innovation Process. Now we have to put faces and names to those Most Important Customers. We suggest you start with a list of 24. You need a total of 12, i.e., six pairs of interviewees.

Name	Title	Company	Location	Phone #	Email address	Back up contact

Company and location are important because you need to be sensitive to competitive issues and time zones. If we were recruiting residential paint contractors, it would be advisable to recruit from different parts of the country but in the same time zone, e.g., Boston and Fort Lauderdale. If we were recruiting department merchandisers, we know we will not be able to recruit a department merchandiser from Walmart and Carrefour to participate in the same interview but we probably would be able to recruit a pair from Walmart or Carrefour who have responsibility for a different department or come from different areas of the country. The team should be involved in drawing up the final list.

Ideally the lead interviewer should call the potential candidates and use page 1 of the interview instrument to explain why he/she is calling. The recruiter should be ready to answer any questions: How long will an interview take? Why will there be two people? What's in it for me? What time are we likely to do this? How long will the whole process take? Will you send me pre-read material?

Is recruiting Most Important Customers easy? No. We did some work for a major paint company and had to contact 200 residential paint contractors to get 11 acceptances.

We have often heard, "But this is hard work." We respond, "Yes, it can be. Have you developed a gold mine? It takes years. Yours will only take weeks!" The outputs from the interviews with the 11 paint contractors were worth their weight in gold. Be prepared to make it happen.

If the Most Important Customer is internal to your organization, recruiting should be much easier.

Once you have completed setting up the 6 first round interviews, most of the pain is over. Scheduling the 2nd and 3rd rounds of interviews is much easier.

If you have a long list of target companies (e.g., 100 or more) that are current, and Most Important Customers, how do you boil the list down? You use Whitney's rules (7) (See Figure 37).

- 20% of your customers generate 80% of your profits
- Companies typically invest equivalent time in all customers
- Need to focus on the 20%

Whitney has three questions you need to ask about your customers:

A. Is your customer strategically significant in their market(s)? Yes or No
B. Does your customer buy a lot of your products and services? Yes or No
C. Do you deliver strong margins off your business with this customer? Yes or No

This produces **8 different customer types**:

Figure 37: Whitney's Rules – 8 Different Customer Classifications

8 Classes of Customer

Class	1	2	3	4	5	6	7	8
A	Yes	Yes	No	Yes	Yes	No	No	No
B	Yes	Yes	Yes	No	No	Yes	No	No
C	Yes	No	Yes	Yes	No	No	Yes	No
Interview		?			↑	Fire	↑	Fire

Want to interview Customers in Classes 1, 3 and 4

Should fire those in Classes 6 and 8

John Whitney, "Strategic Renewal for Business Units, HBR, July-August, 1996, pp 84-98

You should interview customers in classes 1,3 and 4.

Setting up the telecon platform: Identify who you are going to use: ReadyTalk, Webex, GoToMeeting, other. Whoever you select, they must be able to provide the following:

➢ Toll free call-in numbers (not only for the US but other countries around the world)

- The ability to record audio/video and download and allow you to download the recording to your server
- Provide immediate help if there's a problem. This is where we find Webex and GoToMeeting lacking. When you call 1-800-843-9166, ReadyTalk will respond within 30 seconds 7/24.

Using the platform; walking through the 1st round interview; role of the lead interviewer and scribes:

The lead interviewer or one of the scribes should be fully comfortable operating the platform. That person must make sure you are in record mode and help interviewees log on. Those first two or three minutes can be a disaster if that person is uncomfortable with the technology. It sets the tone for what is to follow. This is the most important part of the interview: The lead interviewer's job is to establish credibility and trust. At the same time he/she must make the interviewees feel comfortable.

The lead interviewer needs to know how he/she is going to do to "break the ice" and win the confidence and trust of the interviewees in the first 30 to 60 seconds. It might be a news event, a piece of sports news or trivia, weather, whatever seems natural. The interviewees need to be comfortable when they hear the first question. We like to lead off with "What keeps you awake at night?"

You will now understand why the lead interviewer must be able to function well in this environment. The lead interviewer must listen intently and be ready to react with follow up questions to the unexpected, or unclear, answer.

The Lead Interviewer explains who is on the call and why, as well as the roles they will be playing. He/she will explain how the questions will be asked: "I will ask interviewee 1 the first question and then ask interviewee 2 the same question. I will stay with interviewee 2 for the second question and then come back to interviewee 1 for the answer to the second question. At that point I will ask the scribes and others on the call if they have any clarifying questions." It is very important that each question is directed to the interviewee by name. Remember, this is all audio and people may not be familiar with each other. Most importantly, the person who is doing the transcription needs to be aware of who is responding.

The lead interviewer is in control of the interview at all

times. The ratio of interviewer/interviewee time talking ideally is 5/95 and certainly no more than 10/90. Scribes and others on the call do not interrupt. The lead interviewer will give them time to ask for clarification or ask a question.

Wrapping up, next steps, objectives for the 2nd round, winning commitment from interviewees:

Thank the interviewees for their proactive participation and ask them to rate the value of the past hour to them on a 1-5 scale (1 = V Poor; 5 = Exceptional). The responses typically are in the 4 or 5 range. There will be some "3"s . They will share they really saw value in this but need to see the results of this effort before rating it higher.

We hear frequently, "It has really helped me. I have never been asked these questions before and it's forced me to think about what I do and how I do it."

We also hear, "It was great to have somebody else on the call with me. Now I know there is somebody out there facing the same challenges." In one case, the two interviewees became friends and have visited each other. Have the interviewees share what they liked, and what they didn't like and what could be done to improve the process. Confirm the date and time for the second round interview for two to three weeks out.
Remember we need to complete the 10-Step Process in 3 months or less, this process cannot drag on for months or even years.

Analyzing the 1st round outputs:

Downloading the recordings: Download the recordings to your server and make it available to all team members.

Transcribing the recordings: You have two options here –

1. Do it internally using Dragon software
2. Contract with a transcription service.

Transcribing within your organization is time consuming and expensive. Transcription services are far more accurate, they are court reporters. They will complete a 1 hour interview in less than 2 days for US$250 or less. Just provide them with the URL.

We have used Verbalink out of Santa Monica, CA and they are excellent: http://www.verbalink.com/

Highlighting the transcripts (How, who, what do with the highlights):

1st Step: Download the recording and store in data central. This is particularly useful for team members who join the team later. They can listen to all these interviews.

2nd Step: The transcript back from Verbalink will be a .docx file, 30 to 40 pages in length. Store the transcript in data central.

3rd Step: Put the transcript into a standard template with links. The links will help you move back and forth through the document much more easily. Here are some suggested headers for your template:

- Front Page
- Table of Contents
- Interview details (Date, Time, Interview team, Interview Leader, Interviewes with their contact information)
- The 1st Round interview questions
- Introductions
- Questions and answers (highlight the 1st round questions in the text)
- Wrap Up and feedback
- Tentative date and time for the 2nd interview.

4th Step: Set up a template in .xlsm that will allow you to capture highlighted comments from the transcript and enter them under one of three headers:

- Elements of Performance (take these from your "As Is" Value Curve with Metrics) – Elements of Performance (each EoP must be listed in the file);
- New Elements of Performance (Elements that are relevant to your project but you had not thought of) – New EoP;
- Out of Scope (Comments that you feel are important and should be captured but are clearly out of scope for your project) – OOS. There are potential nuggets here. Make

sure this "Tab" is forwarded to the decision makers and influencers in your organization.

You also need to capture comments by interviewer and interviewee so that if you need to go back and ascribe a comment to a particular interviewee, you can do so relatively easily.

5th Step: Have two people from the interview team go through the interview and highlight relevant comments.

- After each highlight, enter whether it's an Element of Performance (EoP), New Element of Performance (New EoP) or Out of Scope (OOS).
- Enter the name of the EoP or new EoP at the end of the highlight. The first person completes this process using one highlight color and then forwards the document to the second person to repeat the process using a different highlight color.
- The second person only addresses unhighlighted text unless he/she disagrees with a highlighted section.
- Highlight a complete sentence or a paragraph, not a couple of words. It's important to keep the thought captured in the context that it was delivered.

Note: If you have six people on the team, we suggest you have three pairs doing this and do two interviews/pair. This spreads the work load. Each interview will take from 60 to 90 minutes to complete and you will land up with 30 to 50 highlighted comments/interview.

6th Step: Copy and paste the highlighted comments into the master .xlsm file. Total time for this will be 1 hour/interview (A total of 6 hours). The total number of comments captured will be at least 250 and could be as high as 350 to 400. There is a wealth of information in this file. If you have set up the template the right way you will automatically get a citation count for each Element of Performance (EoP), New Element of Performance (New EoP) and all Out of Scope OOS. This will allow you to generate a bar graph showing total number of citations by EoP and New EoP (See Figure 38). One of our clients prefers to call citations, "Nuggets". This will be your first look at rank ordering through the eyes of the Most Important Customer.

Figure 38: Citation count for each Element of Performance

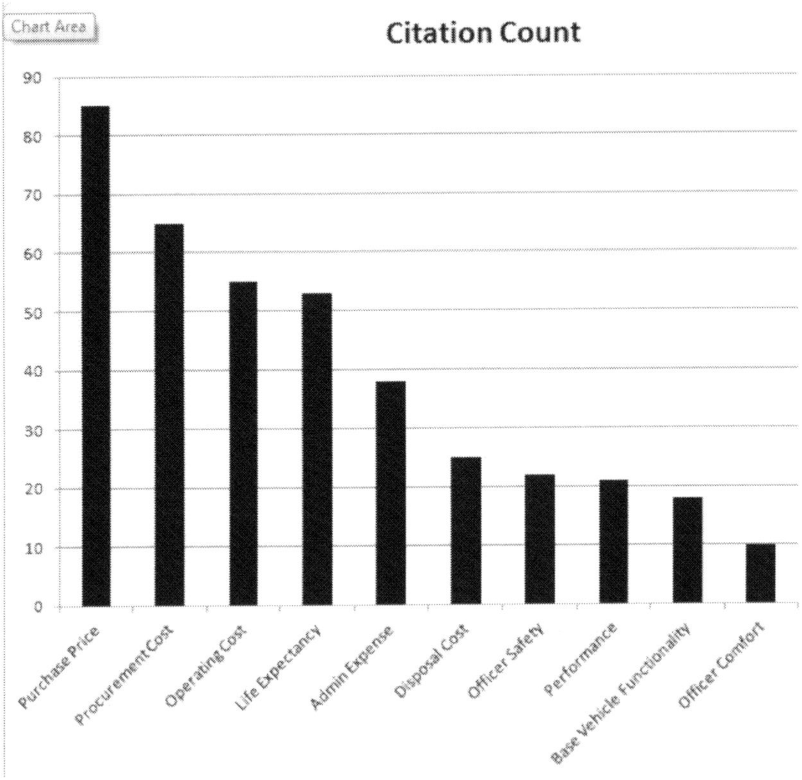

This is now becoming very exciting. You have put in a lot of work to get to this point. Now you are seeing the reward. You have moved into a new world. No longer are you responding to a request made in a two minute conversation between one of your salespeople and a customer at a Las Vegas or a Frankfurt trade show. You are now looking at the combined output from 6 hours of well planned interviews and discussion between 12 subject matter experts.

Reviewing the .xlsm files
(interviewee comments listed by Element of Performance):

The team needs to meet and review the overall findings. The team should agree on:

- The New Elements of Performance (EoPs) that should be added to the "As Is" Value Curve
- Elements of Performance (EoPs) that should be removed from the "As Is" Value Curve
- Rank order change of the Elements of Performance (EoPs) and New Elements of Performance (New EoPs)
- Changes to the value being delivered on each Element of Performance EoP

The output at this point is a revised version of the "As Is" Value Curve with Metrics.

How does Contextual Interviewing fit with Focus Groups and Voice of the Customer?

Focus groups: Focus Groups are being conducted differently today. This new approach has addressed the following drawbacks:

- Takes Most Important Customers out of their environment
- Group members do not know each other
- The most assertive member(s) dominate
- Outputs provide incremental improvements to existing products or services
- Expensive

Procter and Gamble's Consumer Village at one of their R&D facilities in Cincinnati (See Figure 39) provides the following advantages:

- They keep the groups intact, they keep bringing back the same groups
- It becomes a meeting of friends
- They use round tables with multiple P&G facilitators – there are no one-way mirrors
- It is easy to do

Figure 39: Consumer Village is housed in this P&G R&D facility in Cincinnati

Voice of the Customer: Gerry Katz, a Voice of the Customer guru, published "Nine myths about the Voice of the Customer," in October, 2011 (8). This paper is well worth the read. His key takeaways are compared to those described in this book in Figure 40.

Figure 40: Comparison of Voice of the Customer and Contextual Interviewing

Gerry Katz: At the end of the Voice of the Customer process, you will have...	Using the Contextual Interviewing approach described here; you will have...
A detailed list of about 70 to 140 unique customer need statements (that come from about 20 to 40 interviews)	250 to 350 unique citations from 6 interviews with 12 Most Important Customers.
Phrases organized/affinitized (preferably by the customers) into 15 to 25 "buckets" or affinity groupings	Citations are organized into 12 or less Elements of Performance (attributes)
Needs clustered that are prioritized in terms of their relative importance and performance	Unmet needs are prioritized in "As Is" and "To Be" Value Curves with Metrics. The details of these Value Curves are vetted by Most Important Customers in Steps 6-7 of the Value Innovation Process.

As the figure illustrates, Contextual Interviewing yields more results than Voice of the Customer from a smaller number of interviews. Both processes are in depth and take a lot of effort. However, the results are remarkable when carried out properly. It is a truly eye-opening experience. As you continue the process to its conclusion, you will develop higher value new products and services, delight customers and drive sustainable profitable growth.

Next Steps:

1. Select which projects you want to use to pilot the first round of Contextual Interviews:
    - Set up interview team
    - Select the lead interviewer using ISPI or KAI Index
    - Define roles and responsibilities
    - Develop the instrument:
        - Background
        - 6 to 8 questions
        - The wrap-up
    - Draw up a list of 24 Most Important Customers with contact information
    - Recruit 12 interviewees and set up 6 interviewee pairs
    - Schedule the six interviews
    - Use the first interview to pilot the process
    - Make adjustments based on the first interview

2. Conduct all six interviews.
3. Analyze the outputs:
    - Select a transcription service
    - Send the recordings to be transcribed
    - Setup a template to organize the interview transcripts
    - Highlight comments in the transcript. Sort comments by
        - Elements of Performance (EoP)
        - New Element of Performance (New EoP)
        - Out of Scope (OOS)
    - Develop an .xlsm template into which you will enter comments by EoP, New EoP and OOS
    - Enter the highlighted comments into the template
    - Generate a bar graph of # of citations by EoPs, New EoPs, and OOS

4. Store all documents generated in data central.
5. Share all Out of Scope comments with senior management.
6. You are now ready to go to Step 5 of the Value Innovation Process.

Takeaways:

1. You need to understand the jobs your products and services are hired to do.
2. Marketing has few tools for ferreting out the unarticulated needs of customers.
3. Contextual Interviewing is the most important thing your company can do to generate sustainable top line growth. Contextual Interviewing is the single most important activity in the Value Innovation Process. This is the single most important tool you have in the development of new products and services. Get this wrong and everything else in the development cycle will be wrong.
4. The better you plan the interviewing process, the better the results
5. There are three separate interviews, occurring over a 4 to 6 week period. The goals for the three interviews are different.
6. You will learn more with two interviewees than with one or three interviewees.
7. The interview team must have all key functional areas must be represented.
8. Selecting your Lead Interviewer is critically important. There are at least two tools to help you make that selection: ISPI or KAI Index.
9. Record all interviews, transcribe them and store them on a server that all project team members can access.
10. Establish access rights to data central. The future of your company sits in data central.
11. Carry these interviews out over the phone. It is the least expensive, most convenient and least obtrusive way to carry out contextual interviews.
12. It takes a lot of effort and time to do this right. You are mining for gold, it is worth the effort!

Chapter 6

"Our challenge at P&G is to innovate how we innovate."

A G Lafley, retired chairman and CEO, Procter and Gamble

Value Innovation Process Step #5:

Develop the "To Be" Value Curve, Rank Order the Elements of Performance, Develop metrics for each Element

In step #4 of the Value Innovation Process we uncovered the Most Important Customer's unmet needs. In Step #5, we take the "As Is" Value Curve we developed in Step #3, the unmet needs from Step #4 and the Six Questions to define the "To Be" Value Curve.

<table>
<tr>
<td>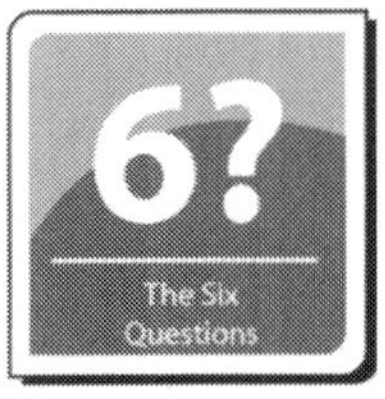
</td>
<td>

What are the 6 Questions?

1. What element(s) of performance should you decrease the value delivered, or eliminate?
2. What element(s) of performance should you increase the value delivered?
3. What new element of performance should you introduce that was uncovered in Step 4?
4. Do these changes make the value proposition for the Most Important Customer compelling?
5. Is this position unique?
6. Do you need to/ can you defend this position?

</td>
</tr>
</table>

Here is the logic to follow using: the 6 Questions, The "As Is" Value Curve with Metrics from Step 3 and The outputs from the 1st Round of Contextual Interviews carried out in Step 4.

1. What elements of performance should you decrease in value delivered after the first round of Contextual Interviews?
   - Should certain Elements of Performance be eliminated?
   - What Elements of Performance are no longer as important?

2. What element of performance should you increase in value delivered after the first round of Contextual Interviews?
   - Are there Elements of Performance where you should increase the value delivered?
   - Pay particular attention to the top 3 or 4 Elements of Performance. This is where you deliver the greatest value to the Most Important Customer.

3. Is there a new element of performance that should be introduced as a result of the first round of interviews?
   - These Elements will come from the Most Important Customer's unmet, unarticulated needs uncovered in the 1st Round of interviews.

4. Do the changes we have made in 1, 2, and 3 above make the value proposition for the Most Important Customer compelling?
   - You will have some feeling for the answer to this question at this point. More will appear after the 2nd round of Contextual Interviews.
   - If the answer is "No", go back to questions 1 through 3 and address them again. If the answer is still "No", cancel the project.
   - If the answer is "Yes", proceed to question 5.

5. Is this position unique?
   - Will you be able to differentiate your product, service, business model, packaging, delivery, offering in the marketplace? If the answer is "Yes", proceed to question 6.

6. Can you defend this position?

The fundamental takeaway here: If the answer to questions 4, 5 and 6 is "Yes", you have defined a Blue Ocean.

The following case studies demonstrate how to apply the Value Innovations tools in Step 6.

	Company	Product or Service
1	FoldedPak	ExpandOS Packaging material replacing bubble wrap, foam in place and Styrofoam peanuts
2	Samsung	LCD TVs in the US market

FoldedPak - ExpandOS™

We shared the FoldedPak ExpandOS case study in Chapters 2 and 4. You will recall ExpandOS is a packing material cut from recycled cardboard, folded and crimped into a pyramid that is a replacement for bubble wrap, chips, foam in place, or Styrofoam Peanuts. This world class product was invented in 2003. The US patent has been filed in 20 countries.

FoldedPak was founded in 2004. By September, 2009, the company was on the verge of bankruptcy after $7 million of venture capital had been invested.

ExpandOS worked very well. Locked inside a box (Block and Brace) it was the most protective and most environmentally friendly packing material in the world. Produced from recycled cardboard, the product is 100% recyclable and no damage occurs in shipping. To demonstrate this, the company ships a brick, two ceramic coffee mugs and two light bulbs packed with ExpandOS in a 12"x12"x12" box.

In 2004, the company chose to sell to industrial packing users through distributors. This industrial market segment views any new products with a skeptical eye.

The ExpandOS "As Is" Value Curve with Metrics compared to Styrofoam Peanuts is shown in Figure 41. Peanuts delivered greater value than ExpandOS on Total Cost, Ease of Use and Product Cost. Peanuts deliver less value on Damage in Delivery but in void fill applications, this is not an issue for manufacturers.

Figure 41: "As Is" Value Curve for ExpandOS

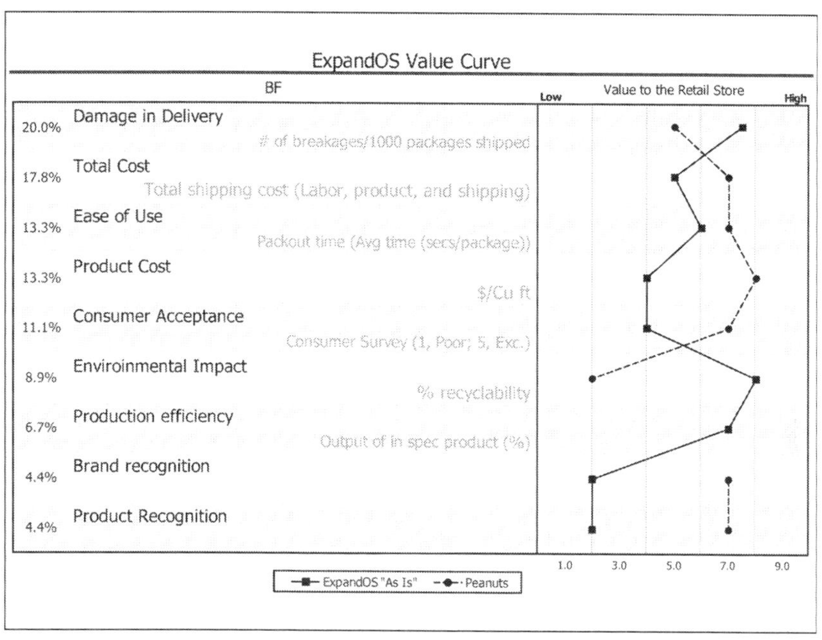

You will recall Brad Fehn, Managing Director of Duart Capital, was brought in as the interim CEO to see if the business could be saved. As a result of Brad's analysis and the results of contextual interviews from Step 4, there were four major conclusions:

1. ExpandOS's cost needed to be reduced
2. Machine efficiencies to produce ExpandOS needed improvement
3. On the B2C side of the Value Chain, ExpandOS could be attractive to consumers. This was a market that FoldedPak had not explored,
4. On the B2B side of the Value Chain, FoldedPak needed to focus on manufacturers of high value added, fragile products

The conclusions from the first round of contextual interviews carried out in Step 4 with Most Important Customers are summarized in Figure 42:

Figure 42: Conclusions from Step 4 of the Value Innovation Process

Three of the 6 Questions	Action
1. What element of performance should the value delivered be decreased?	➢ None
2. What element of performance should be increased in the value delivered?	Reduce ➢ Product Cost ➢ Delivered Cost ➢ Packout Time
3. What new element of performance or service could be introduced that has not been thought of before?	➢ None

Here are the results from FoldedPak's new focus:

Reduce manufactured cost and improve machine efficiency:

- The quality of the cut paper/cardboard stack was improved and machine reliability was increased by reducing incidents/mo. from 4 to 1.
- Different quality feedstock was developed to produce a range of products (e.g., Low Cost – Lower Protection; Higher Cost – Block and Brace), see Figure 43.

Figure 43: ExpandOS products for the industrial market

Application	Product	Price ($/cu ft) to an industrial end user
Low Cost – Lower Protection	Peanuts	0.80 – 1.00
	ExpandOS	0.80 – 1.00
Higher Cost – Block and Brace	ExpandOS	2.50 – 3.50

Demonstrate the effectiveness of ExpandOS:

FoldedPak invested time to develop relationships with mass merchants and big box retailers who recognized the value of an environmentally acceptable packaging material and potential attractiveness to the consumer. The results are illustrated in Figure 44.

Figure 44: ExpandOS successes in the retail market

	# of stores	Start Up	Retail Price	Manufacturer (Cut Paper)	Distributor (Fold and Crimp)
Home Depot	400	July, 2011	$6 to $8 /0.75 ft^3	Graphic Packaging	Pratt Industries
Canada Post	2000[a]	4Q, 2011			Crown Hill (Toronto)

a. *Canada Post has 9,000 Postal Service Centers. Canada Post's business will increase FoldedPak revenues by 4x.*

Focus on manufacturers of high value added, fragile products:

With the improvement in machine reliability, the development of a range of products and acceptance in the retail market, the Industrial Market has returned. FoldedPak now has >100 customers. Customers include: Coors Tek, hp, Southern Seasons, National Semi Conductor, Beyond the Rack, 10 Strawberry Street and Paragon Pumps.

The ExpandOS "To be" Value Curve with Metrics is shown in Figure 45.

Figure 45: ExpandOS "To Be" Value Curve

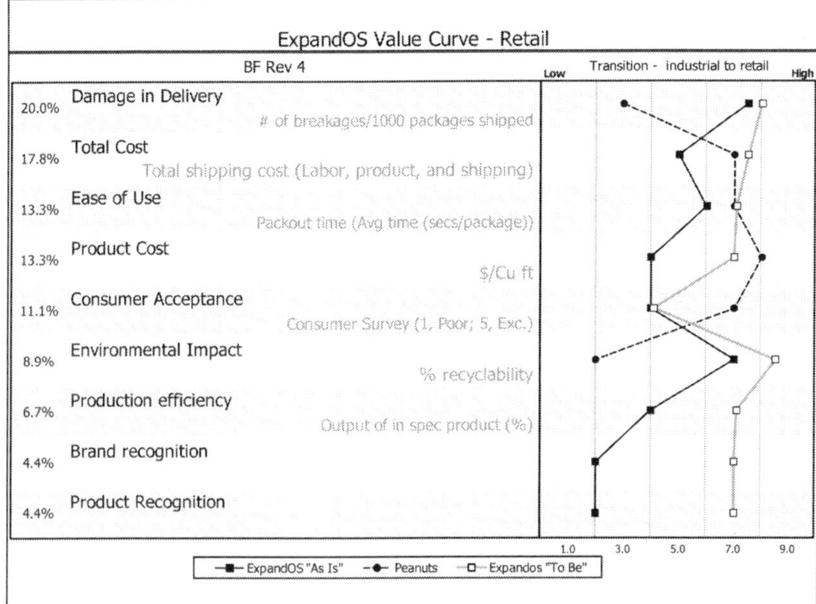

Samsung Electronics:

Samsung Electronics was a "Rule Taker" in 1993. They have transitioned to a "Rule Maker" today, sharing this role with Apple. Samsung, like Apple, understands how to deliver exceptional value to their Most Important Customers, the consumer.

Samsung Electronics Co., Ltd. is a global leader in

semiconductor, telecommunication, digital media and digital convergence technologies. In 2011 Samsung had consolidated sales of US$146.8 billion (up 7% from 2010). Employing approximately 190,500 people in 206 offices across 68 countries, the company operates two separate organizations to coordinate its nine independent business units. They are: Digital Media & Communications, comprising Visual Display, Mobile Communications, Telecommunication Systems, Digital Appliances, IT Solutions. The second organization is Digital Imaging; and Device Solutions, consisting of Memory, System LSI and LCD. Recognized for its industry-leading performance across a range of economic, environmental and social criteria, Samsung Electronics was named the world's most sustainable technology company in the 2011 Dow Jones Sustainability Index.

In 1Q, 2012, Samsung overtook Nokia to become largest producer of mobile phones in the world. Apple and Samsung trade the leadership role as market share leader in smart phones. In 1Q, 2012, Samsung sold 44 million smartphones, taking back the #1 market position from Apple.

Samsung Electronics uses Value Innovation Methodology and tools. With the help of W. Chan Kim and Renée Mauborgne in the mid 1990s, they developed the following:

- The Value Innovation Program Center (VIP) in Suwon.
- The training programs used in Samsung's Value Innovation Program Center
- Strategy canvases (value curves). Any major project at Samsung must have a value curve.

Samsung has six design labs, five of them are outside Korea. They have six hundred industrial designers around the world who capture the information gathered from contextual interviewing and translate that information for the engineers. Samsung engineers do not make design decisions. Samsung has rocketed past Sony and Nokia in sales of TVs and mobile phones. A cell phone with new features is released every two weeks. They have reduced the development cycle time on phones from fourteen months to five months.

Samsung's Value Innovation Program Center in Suwon opened in 1998. The first floor is devoted to training: Lean, Value Innovation, Stage-Gate, Portfolio Management, etc. Floors 2 through 4 are dedicated to high priority projects. Each of the 20 rooms (See Figure 46) has a co-located, dedicated project team. The fifth floor has 42 rooms, two beds in each room and a shower. Some project teams do not go home until the project is completed. Samsung provides a kitchen, gym, ping pong, etc. so team members can relax. At the Value Innovation Program Center, they work on everything from new strategies and business models, to new products, new processes to solving manufacturing problems. They have 50 Subject Matter Experts, including Value Innovation, on site who provide training and will work on project teams when requested.

Figure 46: A project team room inside Camp Suwon (1)

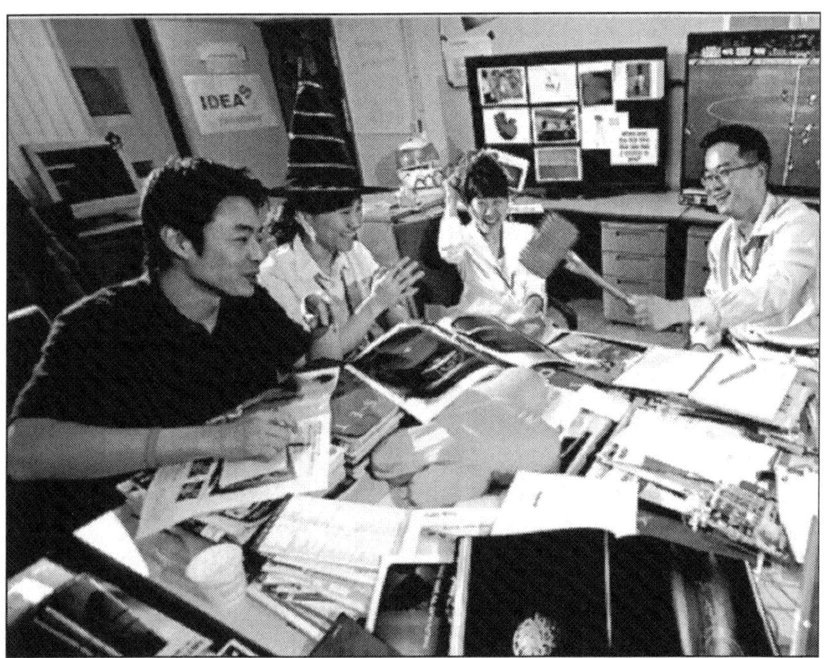

In June, 2005, Samsung set up an eleven person team, including a Value Innovation Specialist. The goal: Increase the sale of LCD TVs in the US by 1 million units. The first task was to develop a value curve that would define the features and design for a flat screen TV for the US market. A facsimile of the "As Is" Value Curve is shown in Figure 47. The most important element of performance to the Most Important Customer, the consumer, was purchase price. The second most important element of performance was picture quality. The third was design for emotional appeal and, the fourth, compatibility with existing furniture.

Figure 47: "As Is" Value Curve for LCD TVs in the US

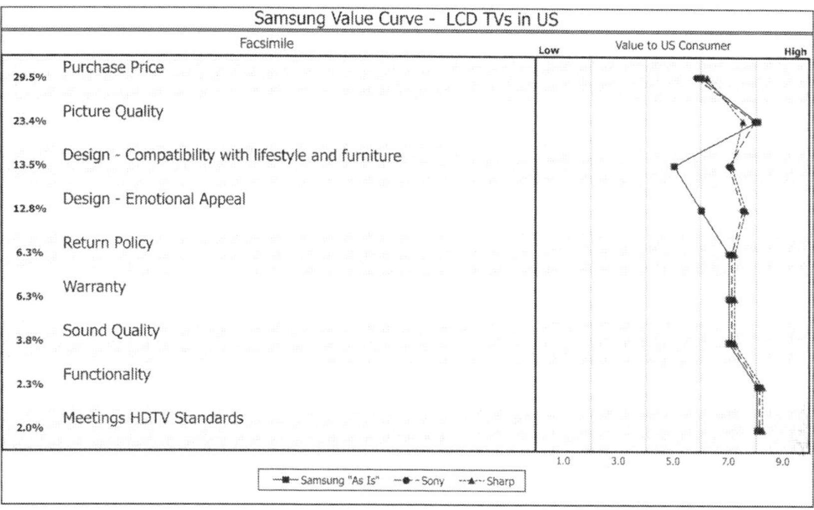

Using the 6 Questions, here are the results:

Three of the 6 Questions	Action
1. What element of performance should be decreased in value delivered? What Elements of Performance can be eliminated?	Decrease the value delivered on: ➢ Sound Quality ➢ Functionality ➢ Meeting HDTV Standards
2. What element of performance should be increased in the value delivered?	➢ Reduce Price ➢ Both Design Elements of Performance
3. What new element of performance could be introduced that has not been thought of before?	➢ None

Since price was the Most Important Element of performance, and the team was going to reduce price, the team committed to minimizing the negative impact on gross margin. The team took cost out by delivering lower value on Sound Quality (lower quality and cost speakers mounted on the back of the TV), Functionality (Reducing the number of features) and Meeting HDTV Standards (they exceeded these standards). They decided not change the value delivered on picture quality as they had a JV with Sony for LCD flat screen production (See Figure 48). Any improvements they made would also accrue to Sony.

Figure 48: The "To Be" Value Curve with Metrics for LCD TVs

Samsung Value Curve - LCD TVs in US

	Facsimile	Low — Value to US Consumer — High
29.5%	Purchase Price	
23.4%	Picture Quality	
13.5%	Design - Compatibility with lifestyle and furniture	
12.8%	Design - Emotional Appeal	
6.3%	Return Policy	
6.3%	Warranty	
3.8%	Sound Quality	
2.3%	Functionality	
2.0%	Meetings HDTV Standards	
		1.0 3.0 5.0 7.0 9.0

Samsung "As Is" · Sony · Sharp · Samsung "To Be"

The team concluded the value proposition to the US consumer would be compelling but did not appear to address questions 5 and 6, i.e., Is the position we are going to take unique? Is that position defensible?

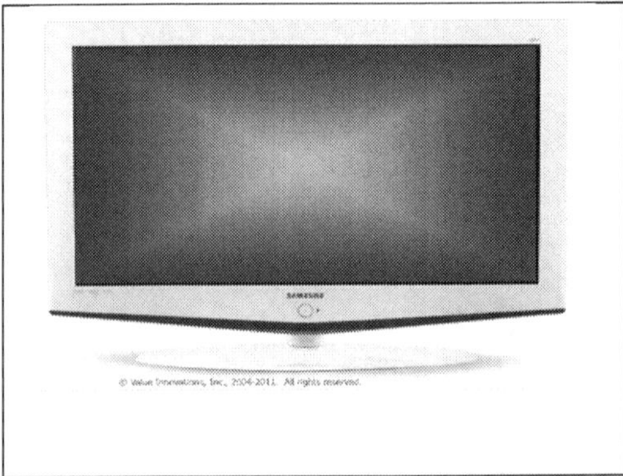

The 51/52 Series TV, later called the Bordeaux, was launched in the US market in February 2006. Development time was completed in five months. Total commercialization time was eight months.

Samsung's US LCD TV market share increased dramatically. More than 2X in five months. They vaulted to #1 in the US, see Figure 49 (2).

Figure 49: Samsung LCD TV Market Share in the US

Company	January, 2006	May, 2006
Samsung	12.1%	26.4%
Sony		24.6%
Sharp		8.4%

Today Samsung Electronics is world's largest manufacturer of TVs and the largest technology company in the world. They have come a long way since 1993.

Next Steps:

1. Teams meet to review the "As Is" Value Curve with Metrics generated in Step 3 and the output from Step 4:
   - Remove Elements of Performance from the original curve that do not appear important to the Most Important Customer
   - Add new Elements of Performance
   - Based on interviewee output:
     - Adjust the rank order of the Elements of Performance
     - Adjust the value delivered for each Element
     - Generate a strawman "To Be" Value Curve
     - Publish a revised Value Curve with Metrics
2. Have various project teams meet, compare notes, share their Value Curves with Metrics, critique same and revise where necessary

You are now ready to move to Step 6 in the Value Innovation Process

Takeaways:

1. The "As Is" and "To Be" Value Curves with Metrics define what you think you need to do to deliver exceptional value to the Most Important Customer. With metrics and absolute values for them, you have turned the subjective and qualitative to the quantitative.
2. In the 2nd Round interview (Steps 6 and 7 of the Value Innovation Process), you will have the interviewees critique the "As Is" and "To Be" Value Curve with Metrics without showing them the Value Curve.

Chapter 7

"It's not the consumers' job to know what they want."

Steve Jobs

Value Innovation Process Steps #6 and 7:

Validate the "To Be" Value Curve with the Most Important Customer (MIC). Revise based on the Most Important Customer's inputs

Preparing for the 2nd Round Interview: Begin with the straw-man "As Is" and "To Be" Value Curve with Metrics from Step 5. The approach in this 2nd Round interview will be entirely different from that used in the 1st Round. We will be asking questions that converge and allow us to shape where we are going. Our goal is to have the Most Important Customers review and critique the Value Curves without showing the interviewee the Curves. Initially this sounds like an impossible task but in reality it is very easy. At this point you have established relationships with each pair of interviewees. They are becoming familiar with the process and enjoy sharing their thoughts.

Using our police car example to remind you of what the Value Curves look like for the Ford Crown Victoria (the "As Is" case) and the Carbon Motors E-7 (the "To Be" case), See Figure 50:

Figure 50: The Ford Crown Victoria Interceptor and Carbon Motors E-7 Police Car Value Curves with Metrics

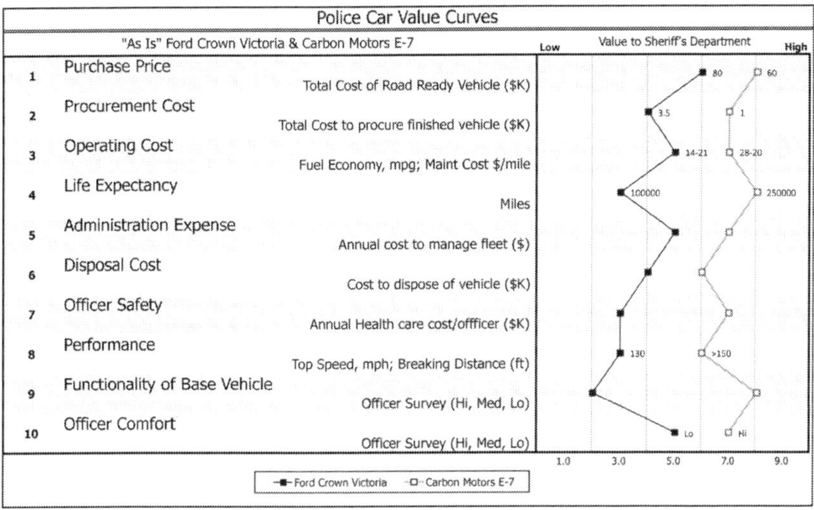

Developing the 2nd Round Instrument: As with the 1st Round there are three major sections:

Introduction - Background
The 6 Questions
Wrap - Up

- **Introduction - Background**
    - Confirm the objectives for the project

- Share the outputs from the 1st Round, e.g., "We carried out six interviews with 12 Subject Matter Experts. We captured 380 citations (comments), sorted them under 12 attributes (we do not use the term Element of Performance, it just introduces confusion) and rank ordered these attributes based on what you shared."
- State the objectives for Round 2: e.g., "We plan to share with you the attributes, their rank order, and the value being delivered to you today for each of those attributes and have you critique them. We will have you review and critique metrics we have developed for each attribute. Finally, we will ask for your thoughts on where value delivered to you should be increased, or decreased."

➢ The 6 questions

1. We developed a list of 10 attributes.

Purchase Price	Officer Safety
Procurement Cost	Life Expectancy
Performance	Operating Cost
Functionality of the base vehicle	Admin Expense
Officer comfort	Disposal Cost

"Does this capture what's important to you in the acquisition and operation of police cars? If not, what should we add? What should we take out?"

We recommend you do not show your interviewees any Value Curves and that you don't use the term Elements of Performance. You simply waste time explaining what these are and you cause confusion.

2. "Would you change the rank order of this list of attributes?"

Attribute	Interviewee 1	Interviewee 2
1. Purchase Price		
2. Procurement Cost		
3. Performance		
4. Functionality of the base vehicle		
5. Officer comfort		
6. Officer Safety		
7. Life Expectancy		
8. Operating Cost		
9. Admin Expense		
10. Disposal Cost		

"If so, what attributes would you move up in order of importance? Why? What would you move down in importance? Why?"

3. "These are the metrics we've developed for these attributes: Are these the right metrics? If not, what should we change?"

Metrics

Attribute	Interviewee 1	Interviewee 2
Purchase Price		
Total cost of road ready vehicle ($K)		
Procurement Cost		
Total cost to procure vehicle ($K)		

Performance		
Top speed (mph); Breaking distance (ft)		
Functionality of the base vehicle		
Officer Survey ((Hi, med, lo)		
Officer comfort		
Officer Survey ((Hi, med, lo)		
Officer Safety		
Annual health care cost/officer ($K)		
Life Expectancy		
Miles		
Operating Cost		
Fuel cost; Maintenance Cost ($/mile)		
Admin Expense		
Annual cost to manage fleet ($K)		
Disposal Cost		
Cost to dispose of vehicle ($K)		

"Could you share with us the absolute value for these metrics, e.g., Is life expectancy for a Ford Crown Victoria 100,000 miles?"

Before moving onto question 4, be sure you have a full/complete definition for each Element of Performance. It is critical that each Most Important Customer understands the terminology.

4. "What value is being delivered to you today on a 1 to 9 scale (1 = Very low Value; 9 = Exceptional Value) on each attribute for your current fleet?"

Current Value Delivered (1 to 9)

Attribute	Interviewee 1	Interviewee 2
Purchase Price		
Procurement Cost		
Performance		
Functionality of the base vehicle		
Officer comfort		
Officer Safety		
Life Expectancy		
Operating Cost		
Admin Expense		
Disposal Cost		

5. "Based on your rank order of these attributes and the value being delivered to you today, where would you want to see the value delivered to you increased? To what value (on our 1 to 9 scale) and why?"

Next Steps:

1. Develop the 2nd Round interview instrument for your pilot projects
   - Assemble your teams
   - Develop the three sections for the instruments
     - Introduction – Background
     - The 6 Questions
     - Wrap-Up
2. Schedule the 6 interviews with the 12 interviewees
   - Record the interviews and store the recordings in data central
3. Document the outputs from Round 2
   - Publish the outputs
   - Revise the "As Is" Value Curve with Metrics
     - Elements of Performance
     - Element rank order
     - Value delivered today for each Element
4. Publish vetted "As Is" and "To Be" Value Curves
5. Have the teams meet, share their Value Curves with Metrics, compare notes, critique same and revise where necessary.

You are now ready to move to Step 8 of the Value Innovation Process

Takeaways:

1. Steps 6-7 of the Value Innovation Process, the 2nd Round of interviews, will provide you with vetted "As Is" and "To Be" Value Curves with Metrics.
2. "As Is" and "To Be" Value Curves make writing a Value Proposition very easy (Step 8 of the Value Innovation Process).

Chapter 8

"The value of achievement lies in the achieving."

Albert Einstein

Value Innovation Process Step #8:

Define the Value Proposition

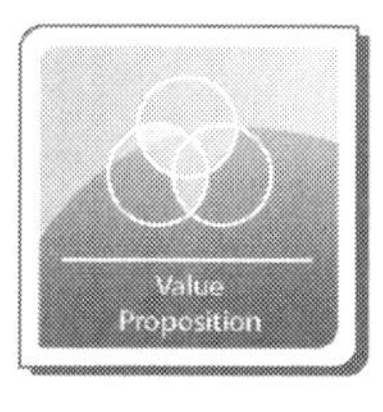

What is a Value Proposition?

The Value Proposition succinctly describes how your product or service will deliver exceptional value to your Most Important Customer(s).

With the "As Is" and "To Be" Value Curve with Metrics you developed in Steps 6 and 7 you are now in a position to define what you are going to do to deliver exceptional value to the Most Important Customer.

Not until you have completed Step 9 can you clearly define "How" you are going to deliver that value. You probably have some good ideas.

The best way to show you how to do this is to share examples. We will first show you the "As Is" and "To Be" Value Curve with Metrics and then write the Value Proposition.

1. The Carbon Motors E-7 Police Car:

Here are the Value Curves with Metrics for the Ford Crown Victoria Interceptor (the "As Is" case) and the Carbon Motors E-7 (the "To Be" case) police cars:

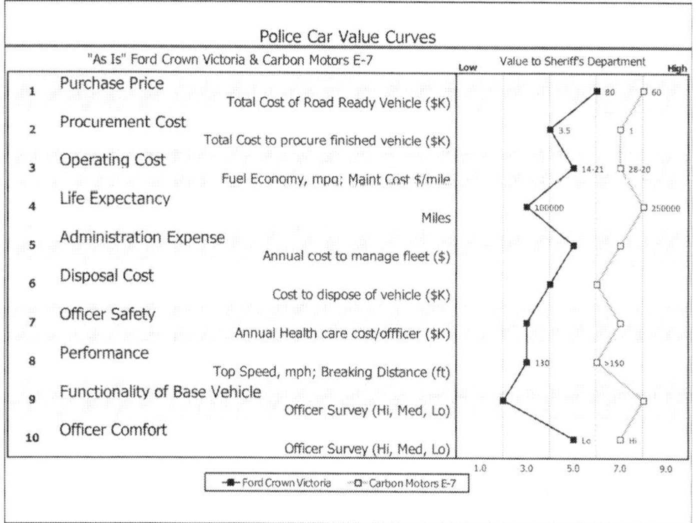

Introducing the E-7:

Value Proposition for the Carbon Motors E-7 Police Car: Built from the ground up to be a law enforcement vehicle, the E-7 is constructed from lightweight materials and powered by a BMW inline-6, turbo-diesel engine. This provides the Sheriff's Department a vehicle with lower procurement, operating, maintenance, administration, and disposal costs; improved fuel efficiency (from 33% to 100%); greater performance (Top speed >150 vs. 130 mph; 0-60mph in 6.5secs); and a life expectancy 2.5 times that of the Ford Interceptor (250,000 miles compared to 100,000 miles). Officer safety and comfort are significantly improved by:

1. 75 mph rear impact crash capability
2. Optional ballistic protection panels
3. Video and audio surveillance of rear passenger compartment
4. Isolated ventilation for front and rear compartments rear
5. Seats designed to accommodate handcuffed suspects/prisoners
6. Rear passenger compartment designed to be hosed down in cleaning
7. Purpose designed seat for use with on-body equipment, seat heating and ventilation.

The purchase price of the E-7 will be the same as, or lower than the road ready Interceptor.

As of April 26, 2012, 20,419 E-7s had been ordered by 587 Agencies in all 50 US States. At a selling price of $80,000/unit, orders for Carbon Motors were US/$1.6 billion. Check out their website to see the latest numbers: http://www.carbonmotors.com/

The Carbon Motors web site provides a laundry list of E-7 features, which is far too long for a Value Proposition. If these were all added to the Value Proposition we would be guilty as charged for not knowing where we were delivering value.

- NIJ Level III-A (or better) ballistic protection (front doors and dash panel)
- Purpose-designed seat for use with on-body equipment and seat heating and ventilation
- Head-up display
- Reverse backup camera
- Remote start capability
- Engine features to enable extended idling as well as operating in extreme conditions (heat and cold)
- Driver-specific intelligent key
- 360 degree exterior surveillance capability, with fully automatic recording
- Automatic license plate recognition system, programmable and upgradeable
- Video and audio surveillance of rear passenger compartment
- Night vision compliant interior illumination
- Integrated forward looking infrared system (FLIR)
- Integrated shotgun and rifle mounts
- Secure weapons storage
- Optimized storage capability (compartment and cargo), to store police gear ranging from spare restraints to forensic equipment
- Integrated front and rear passenger compartment partition
- Isolated ventilation for front and rear compartments
- Rear seats designed to accommodate handcuffed suspects/prisoners
- Security features to prevent escape of prisoners
- Rear passenger compartment designed to be washed by hosing down

- Integrated push bumpers and PIT capability
- Integrated aerodynamic emergency lights with sirens
- The seats are designed for comfort and to reduce back pain while wearing a duty belt

2. Sensodyne Repair and Protect Toothpaste (containing Novamin):

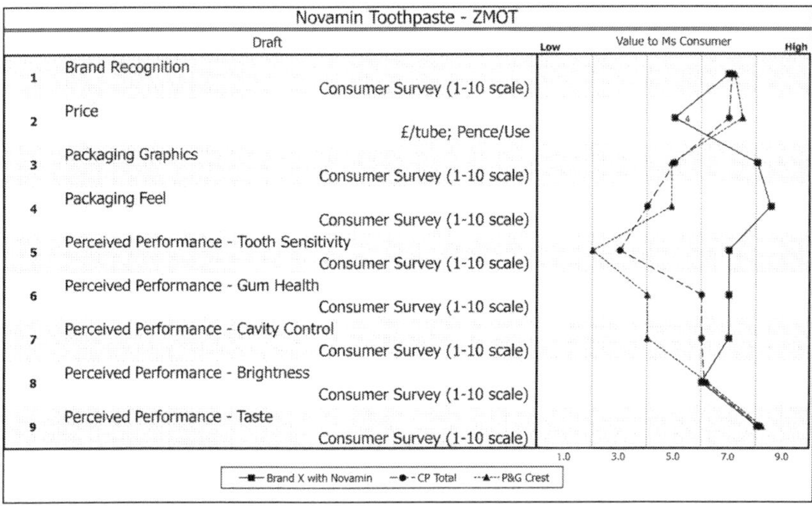

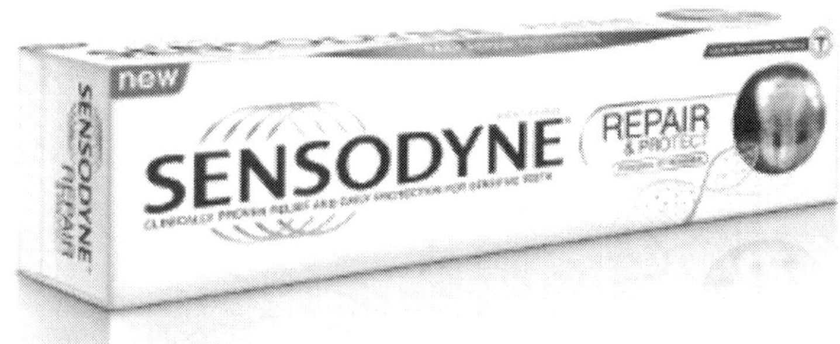

Value Proposition for Sensodyne Repair and Protect:
Repair and Protect is the only toothpaste in the world containing Novamin. Novamin, a bioglass, reacts with saliva to lay down a protective layer on the surface of the tooth thereby repairing and protecting the dentyn layer. As this protective layer builds, tooth sensitivity is reduced. In combination with fluoride, Repair and Protect promotes gum health and controls cavities.
Priced at a premium, Repair and Protect is the fastest growing toothpaste in the world.

Today Repair and Protect is the fastest selling toothpaste in recent memory and, if we read this right, will take the US market when it is introduced.

3. FoldedPak's ExpandOS packaging Material:

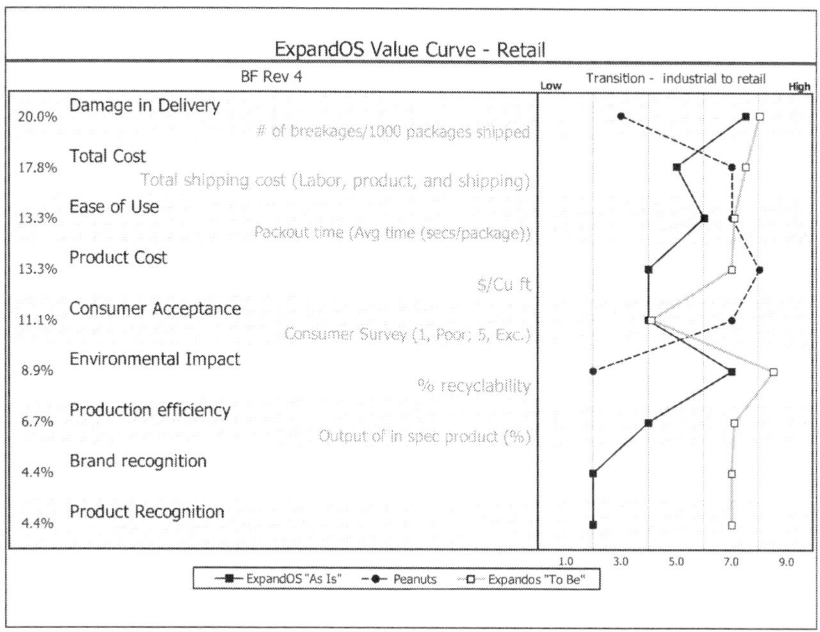

Value Proposition for ExpandOS (to the manufacturer): The patented ExpandOS design locks product in place within the package. This locking feature assures the manufacturer of high value added, fragile products that there will be no damage in transit, provided the external package is not compromised.

Total shipping cost, ease of use and product cost are competitive with alternative packing materials.

Produced from recycled paper and cardboard, ExpandOS is itself 100% recyclable. By using ExpandOS, the manufacturer can demonstrate its commitment to the environment and keeping the planet green.

ExpandOS allows the manufacturer to print its name on each piece of packaging material providing a new avenue for the manufacturer to tell its story.

Next Steps:

1. Take the "As Is" and "To Be" Value Curves with Metrics from Step 7 for your pilot projects and develop a Value Proposition. Focus on the top 3 or 4 Elements of Performance and translate them into what you are going to do to deliver exceptional value to your Most Important Customer.
2. Think about "How" you can deliver the "What". If you are not able to define the "How" at this stage, move to Step 9 and come back to complete the Value Proposition.
3. Meet with the other teams, compare notes, critique each other's Value Propositions, and revise/refine and publish the final Value Propositions.
4. You are now ready to proceed to Step 9.

Takeaways:

1. With "As Is" and "To Be" Value Curves with metrics in hand, it is easy to write a Value Proposition.
2. Waiting until the value proposition is clearly understood helps you focus on what is truly important and not waste time and energy. Waiting to determine the "How" until step 9 is completed is often difficult for the team. It is human nature to want to get started solving problems much earlier in the process.

Chapter 9

"I can't tell you how many product briefs we get saying we want a product that's as good, or better than, the iPhone. That's a five-alarm for me. Those folks don't get it. An iPhone is not a product. It's a manifestation of a culture."

John Barrett, CEO, Teague

Value Innovation Process Step #9:

"How" to deliver the "What"

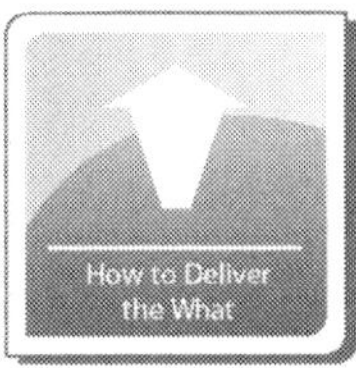

"How" to deliver the "What?"

In our Workshops we use the following process for teams to brainstorm options for the new product or service.

Each team member:

- Has a copy of the "As Is" and "To Be" Value Curves with metrics in front of them
- Writes down his/her ideas on a Post It® Note (one idea/Post It)
- Posts their Post Its up on a flip chart

The teams:

- Review all Post-Its and organize them into groups (these can be Elements of Performance) –Photograph the flip chart.
- Discuss the solutions and develop a list of options, or, define the best solution that shows "How" to deliver the "What"

The ideal situation is three, 4-5 person teams working on this at the same time.
The output (prototype(s) or designs) from this brainstorming will be shared with, and reviewed by, the Most Important Customers in Step 10 of the Value Innovation Process.

In our Mastering Value Innovation Workshops, we have tasked more than two thousand people to transform a commodity into a breakthrough using the 10-Step Value Innovation Process and the brainstorming approach described above. 99% of the attendees have never heard of the company or the product. However within 48 hours, following the steps outlined, these divergent teams reach a similar conclusion to the actual company who did take a commodity product to a breakthrough. It never ceases to amaze us!

1. Brainstorming:

There is nothing new in using brainstorming. There are many companies who can help you brainstorm and lead creativity sessions. Our experience in this instance is that everybody comes up with ideas to address problems when they clearly understand the problem they are trying to solve.

Wikipedia provides all you need for a brief history and the basic ground rules of brainstorming: http://en.wikipedia.org/wiki/Brainstorming.

The following has been excerpted from Wikipedia:

Advertising executive Alex F. Osborn began developing methods for creative problem solving in 1939. He was frustrated by employees' inability to develop creative ideas individually for ad campaigns. In response, he began hosting group-thinking sessions and discovered a significant improvement in the quality and quantity of ideas produced by employees. After organizing his discovery, Osborn published Applied Imagination in 1963 (1) in which he systematized his creative problem-solving methods. This book popularized the term brainstorming and received significant response in the industry.

Osborn claimed that two principles contribute to "ideative efficacy," these being "1. Defer judgment," and "2. Reach for quantity." Osborn had his four general rules of brainstorming, established with intention to reduce social inhibitions among group members, stimulate idea generation, and increase the overall creativity of the group.

1. **Focus on quantity:** This rule is a means of enhancing divergent production, aiming to facilitate problem solving through the maxim quantity breeds quality. The assumption is that the greater the number of ideas generated, the greater the chance of producing a radical and effective solution.
2. **Withhold criticism:** In brainstorming, criticism of ideas generated should be put 'on hold'. Instead, participants should focus on extending or adding to ideas, reserving criticism for a later 'critical stage' of the

process. By suspending judgment, participants will feel free to generate unusual ideas.

3. **Welcome unusual ideas**: To get a good and long list of ideas, unusual ideas are welcomed. They can be generated by looking from new perspectives and suspending assumptions. These new ways of thinking may provide better solutions.
4. **Combine and improve ideas:** Good ideas may be combined to form a single better good idea, as suggested by the slogan "1+1=3". It is believed to stimulate the building of ideas by a process of association. Procter and Gamble has formalized this process with their MIB (Make It Bigger) Meetings.

Osborn notes that brainstorming should address a specific question. By focusing on the "As Is" and "To Be" Value Curves with Metrics, you are doing exactly that. He held that sessions addressing multiple questions were inefficient.

Adopting Osborn's 4 rules for the Value Innovation Process start with the "As Is" and "To Be" Value Curves with metrics. Follow the process we have outlined, with multiple teams for the maximum effect. You will generate a very healthy list of ideas on "How" to deliver exceptional value to your Most Important Customers. Six Thinking Hats, authored by Edward de Bono (2), is a parallel thinking technique used by some companies to focus discussions, reduce meeting length and drive to conclusions. The process is used to manage discussions of ideas surfaced in brainstorming sessions, by fostering a collaborative environment. We have not used this approach to generate "How" to deliver the "What" but could see this being a useful tool for developing solutions to complex problems.

2. Is the position Unique and Defensible?

Review the last three of the 6 Questions.

<table>
<tr>
<td>
</td>
<td>

What are the 6 Questions?

1. What element(s) of performance should you decrease the value delivered, or eliminate?
2. What element(s) of performance should you increase the value delivered?
3. What new element of performance should you introduce that was uncovered in Step 4?
4. Do these changes make the value proposition for the Most Important Customer compelling?
5. Is this position unique?
6. Do you need to/ can you defend this position?

</td>
</tr>
</table>

Since delivering exceptional value to Most Important Customer is our goal, will these changes make the value proposition for the Most Important Customer compelling? If the answer is "yes" we need to address the next two questions:

1. Is this position unique?
2. Do you need to, can you defend this position?

In most cases, you will not know the answer to these questions without more work.

1. What is the patent landscape?
2. How many patents have been issued?
3. Has patent issuance been flat, is it going up, going down?
4. Are there companies or individuals who are very active that could be blockers or potential license partners?, etc.
5. In short we need to conduct a sophisticated patent

search with a company specializing in this area. One of Value Innovations, Inc. partners, Intellectual Assets, Inc. has the core competences required. We recommend you contact Paul Germeraad, Larry Schwartz or Ron Taylor to explore this in more detail.

In 2007 Value Innovations did a case study with Intellectual Assets to demonstrate how this works using gypsum drywall as an example. As you move through each step we think you will get a good sense of what is involved and how critically important this is.

3. Patent Mapping (Using Value Curves and Patent Literature to answer Questions 5 and 6, and Develop Strategic Technology Plans)

Introduction: Part of Dick's career was spent in the building materials industry and had the great experience to work on a new product, Rocklite. The core of this product was expanded low density perlite and sodium silicate, not gypsum. The major difference between Rocklite and regular drywall was weight, Rocklite being 60% lighter. This dramatic reduction in weight resulted in lower freight costs, reduced neck and back injuries, improved sag resistance, and better score & snap capabilities. It also was a natural fire and water barrier, as it is a glass.

Reduced weight is a great advantage but water and fire barrier properties are critical in the built environment. Drywall can be purchased in fire resistant and water resistant forms. It resists water or fire for a limited time. But drywall is not a barrier. If that product could be brought to market, home owners, building owners, and insurance companies would recognize the value and could be willing to pay a premium for the product possibly providing incentives for its use.

With this as background, we decided to step back and look at the drywall industry, ask some high level questions, and draw conclusions about where a drywall company might invest its very limited R&D budget to break out of the commodity business.

Disclaimer: The materials presented and conclusions drawn here have been prepared by Value Innovations, Inc. and Intellectual Assets, Inc. using information in the public domain.

Value Innovations and Intellectual Assets have not consulted with, or obtained information from, any of the drywall manufacturers. The views expressed, and the conclusions drawn, are solely those of Value Innovations and Intellectual Assets and not those of the drywall industry, or any drywall manufacturer.

The materials are being presented to show how Value Innovation methodology and tools, used in combination with a rigorous review of the patent literature, can enable the strategic planning process, enable quality IP decisions, define Blue Ocean Opportunities and drive sustainable, profitable company growth.

We developed and defined: 12 Elements of Performance for wallboard and rank ordered them in order of importance to the general contractor and ultimately, the homeowner/tenant. From this we generated the following "As Is" and "To Be" Value Curves with Metrics for the New Manufacturer and some competitors in the US market: USG, National and Domtar.

Conclusions from the "As Is" and "To Be" Value Curves (See Figure 51):

1. New Mfr "As Is", and competitor's products (USG, National and Domtar) in the US are essentially equivalent.
2. The companies are in a commodity business (swimming in a red ocean) – price, cost and installed capacity are the primary factors determining the players' market share. Product performance and quality are essentially equivalent regardless of the manufacturer.
3. The elements where New Mfr would be advantaged (the "To Be" case) are (in order of importance):
    - Installed cost
    - HSE (personal injury)
    - Fire Barrier
    - Water Barrier
4. Technologies that enable New Mfr to deliver greater value to the general contractor, and subsequently the homeowner/tenant, for the four elements defined in 3 above could potentially:

- ➢ Enable New Mfr to move out of a commodity business
- ➢ Provide New Mfr with "Blue Ocean" Opportunities

Figure 51: "As Is" and "To Be" Value Curves with Metrics for wallboard products

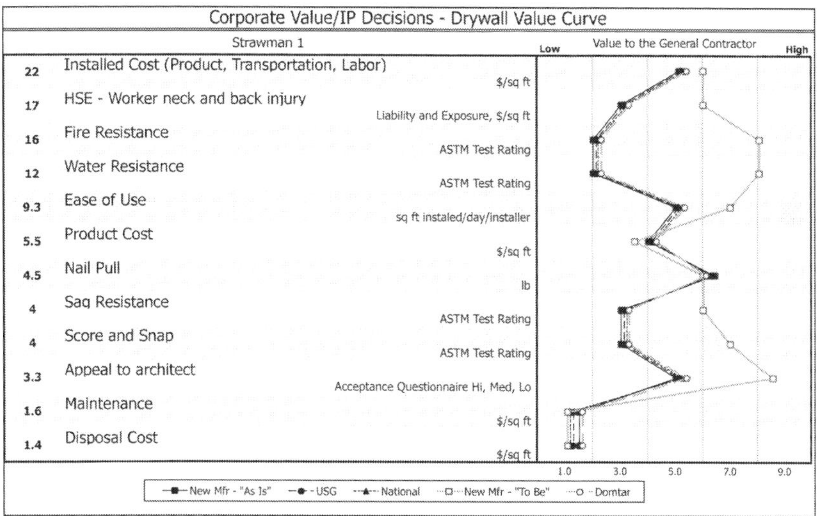

Based on these tentative conclusions, Value Innovations worked with Intellectual Assets to data mine wallboard patent history to answer these questions.

1. Are companies investing in this area?
2. Who are the primary players?
3. Where are the primary investments being made?
4. What does the landscape look like for:
   - ➢ Lowering installed cost
   - ➢ Fire Barrier properties
   - ➢ Water Barrier properties
   - ➢ H,S and E issues
5. For a New Manufacturer interested in wallboard materials
   - ➢ Should an R&D project(s) be initiated?
   - ➢ Are there external technology sources that should be tapped?

- Is there IP that will allow/not allow freedom to proceed?
- Is there IP that will influence an ability to exclude competition (can we defend the unique position we take)?

In 2007, IP databases were searched for drywall and wallboard patents and patent applications issued world-wide & in the US. At that time there were:

- 2000 patents and applications worldwide
- 1400 U.S. patents and applications

Here is the sequence we followed:
U.S. patents were segmented to identify year of issue. We observed:

- This area has attracted new investment over the last decade
- The level of investment has appeared to recently flatten

...and concluded:

- Companies view this commercial area worthy of further R&D investment
- The field looks ready for a breakthrough product
- A company entering the field will have to devote enough resources to review 10 – 15 patent documents/mo.

US art was:

1. Segmented to identify top technologies & uses, We observed:
    - Most art is categorized by use
    - The composition art is modest
    - Process art is also present

...and concluded there is an opportunity to develop and build protection around new fire and water barrier compositions

2. Segmented to identify top cited-by art. We observed:
    - Most top art is focused on application / installation problems
    - The composition art has only modest cited-by rates

...and concluded:

- There is limited IP activity around drywall compositions
- Entry into the field will allow follow-on work to be conducted and funded at industry standard levels

3. Segmented to identify the top assignees by document count and observed:
    - Most work is being done by independents
    - Companies present are those expected from market research
    - There are few academic entities to partner with
    - There is no "statistically special" inventor to contend with
    - There are a number of inventors with modest IP portfolios

...and concluded:

- Independent inventors will be a potential source of innovation
- A new product will invite competition from well funded, entrenched companies

4. Mapped to determine the overall IP landscape (each point on this map is a patent). The first time you see one of these, it looks like a topographical map, and that is a good way to think about it.

Figures 52 and 53 show the detailed Patent Map for wallboard and the overall subjects covered by each area in the map.

Figure 52: Patent Map for Wallboard produced by Intellectual Assets, Inc.

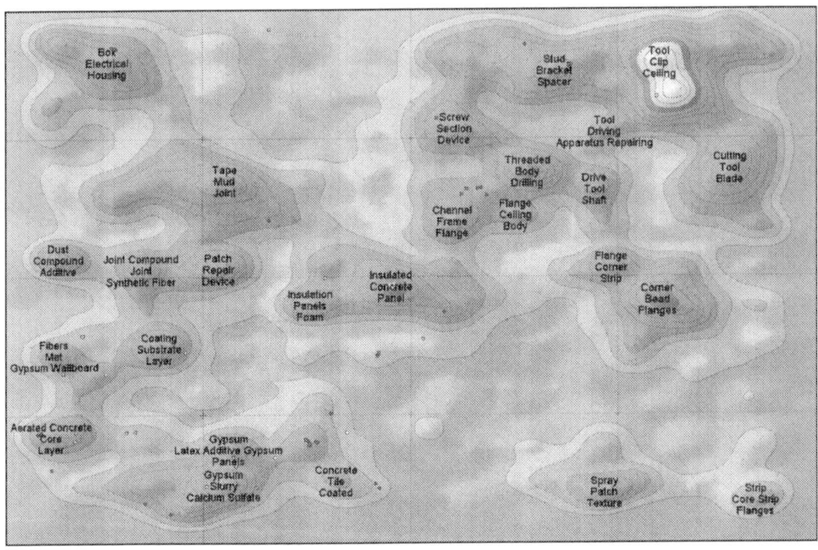

Figure 53: Patent Map showing subjects covered:

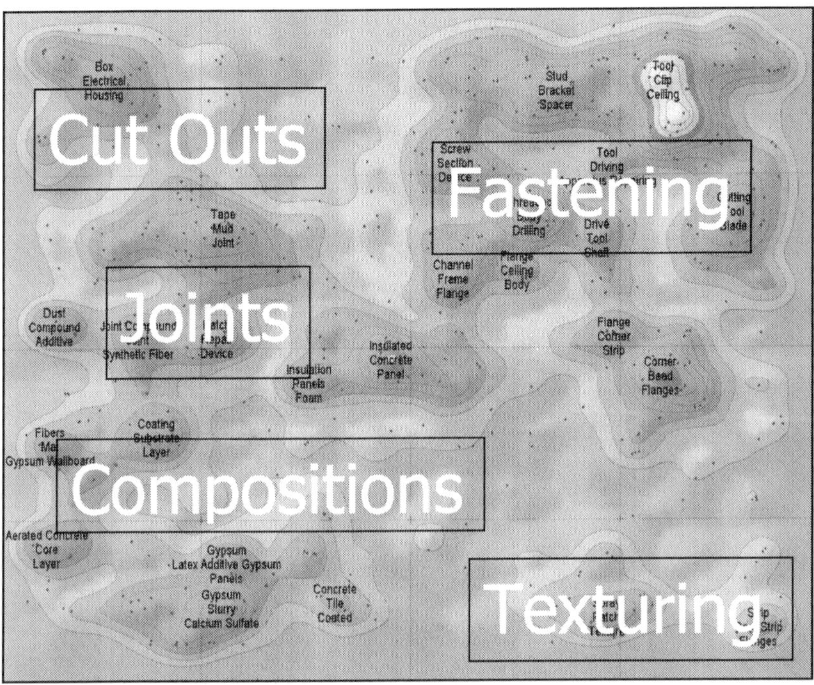

We observed:

- The major areas of drywall composition and installation are heavily covered
- No large area of the landscape is devoted to fire and water barrier properties
- There is significant IP "White Space" to be explored in this field

...and concluded:

- Although this is an overall IP "Forest", the area of fire and water barrier properties appear to be an IP "Desert"
- Fire and water barrier properties art is not located in just one discrete area
- There are only four documents mentioning both fire and water resistance

At the end of this investigation of the patent landscape and patent map, we concluded:

- There is no single approach to fire and water barriers
- There are few apparent efforts to address both issues
- The field is ready for a next generation or breakthrough product
- Fire And Water Resistance combinations are open for innovation
- There are a few companies, inventors and universities that might speed R&D and should be tapped
- Value Curves with Metrics focused the IP investigation onto art most likely to have commercial impact
- There is not likely to be IP that will exclude an ability to work in this area
- There is No "Must-have" or "Feared" inventor

If a company wanted to invest in technologies that could enable water and fire barrier wallboard, it could have a unique product and the company could defend that position.

4. Reinvention Workshops

In chapter 3 we looked at the Value Web for Alcan Pharmaceutical Packaging. The project was "Physicians' Pharmaceutical Samples" - Helping the patient take the right drug at the right time." Using the Value Innovation Process Alcan concluded the patient was the Most Important Customer but that the pharmacy, the physician, and the pharmaceutical company were key influencers. They were key in the decision making process.

Patient "trust" in the medication and in the physician were key findings early in the process. The packaging for the samples had the opportunity to play a key role in establishing that trust. In some cases when the samples had been removed from the packaging by the physician to save space in the office, the samples actually worked against establishing trust.

As Alcan moved into Step 9 of the Value Innovation Process they decided to involve the pharmaceutical company in the process through a Reinvention Workshop. We think this was a first. The goal: Immerse them in the Value Innovation Process and win their "buy-in." Alcan needed the pharmaceutical company to understand the Value Innovation Process and the key findings to convince them how powerful this approach could be. They knew, if successful it could be a very powerful tool to co-create future solutions and give Alcan access to key decision makers that they would normally not meet.
Here is the agenda Alcan used for the day:

1. Overview of Pharmaceutical Sample Landscape (Workshop leader)
2. Sharing of Key Global Trends that might change the business (All, 15 minutes)
3. Overview of Value Innovation (Workshop Leader, 40 Minutes)
   a. Introduction to the tools we will be using today
   b. Blue Ocean Strategy and Alcan's Value Innovation Process
      1. The Value Chain/Web - Why this is important?
      2. Introduction to Value Curves
         - Examples of a Blue Ocean approach
   c. Re-invention case study

4. Sharing of "Must Haves" (The highest rank ordered Elements of Performance)
5. Creation of Pharmaceutical Sample Value Chain/Web
    a. Identify key Elements of importance to each critical part of the value chain/web
6. Break
7. Creating Value Curves (All, 45 minutes)
    a. Current including competition
    b. Future Target ("To Be") Value Curves
8. Brainstorming in groups key elements from the value curve "How might we" (All, 45 min)
9. Report outs from the groups
10. Creation of the follow-up items

Feedback from those attending the Reinvention Workshop.... Outstanding.

5. TRIZ

TRIZ (pronounced TREEZ) is the Russian acronym for the Theory of Inventive Problem Solving. This proven algorithmic approach to solving technical problems began in 1946 when the Russian engineer and scientist Genrikh Altshuller studied thousands of patents and noticed certain patterns. From these patterns he discovered that the evolution of a technical system is not a random process, but is governed by certain objective laws. These laws can be used to consciously develop a system along its path of technical evolution - by determining and implementing innovations. One result of Altshuller's theory -- that inventiveness and creativity can be learned -- has fundamentally altered the psychological model of creativity. TRIZ, developed in the Soviet Union, moved underground after Altshuller was imprisoned for his "heretical" work, until the fall of the USSR. TRIZ re-emerged and migrated to the West. Today many Fortune 500 companies successfully use TRIZ methodology.

The Altshuller Institute for TRIZ Studies is a 501(c) (3) Non-Profit organization (http://www.aitriz.org/) that exists for the benefit of those who:

- Know the TRIZ Methodology,
- For those who want to learn TRIZ, and
- Wish to export TRIZ for the benefit of all mankind.

The Institute is the only organization officially authorized by Genrikh Altshuller, the founder of TRIZ, to use his name.

We have not used TRIZ and are not aware of companies who have used TRIZ in combination with the Value Innovation Process but we feel we should make you aware of the tool.

Next Steps:

1. Identify the tools you will use to develop the "How" to deliver exceptional value to your Most Important Customer.
2. Define the solutions to your Most Important Customers unmet needs.
3. Develop the materials you will share with the Most Important Customers in Step 10, the third and final round of contextual interviews.

Takeaways:

1. Use TRIZ to identify potential solutions to the problems you need to solve.
2. Use subject matter experts not on the project team to develop options on "How to deliver exceptional value to the Most Important Customer"
3. Use accepted brainstorming techniques.
4. Use de Bono's Six Thinking Hats to focus discussions, foster collaboration and reduce the length of, and number of, meetings.
5. Use patent mapping to determine what options you have to develop, buy, or license in technology to develop a unique and defensible position

Chapter 10

"WOW!"

Value Innovation Process Step #10:

The 3rd Contextual Interview – Confirm with the Most Important Customer that the "How" is Compelling

Preparing for the 3nd Round Interview: Bring together the outputs from Steps 6 & 7, the vetted "As Is" and "To Be" Value Curve with Metrics, the Value Proposition developed in Step 8, and the options developed in Step 9. The approach in this 3rd Round interview will be entirely different from those used in the 1st and 2nd Rounds.

You will be:

- Presenting the options developed in Step 9 to the interviewees,
- Explaining how each option functions or works and differs from the others,
- Sharing how each option addresses the top 3 or 4 Elements of Performance from the Value Curve with Metrics
- Describing how each option delivers the "To Be" value for each Element
- Sharing with them how the options would be priced or if you cannot share a price at this point, provide a range. You can also elect not to do this. In the circumstance where the Most Important Customer is a user of your product or service but not the buyer, you probably would not address price at this point.

You will ask the interviewees to critique the options, and have them share which option they like most and the reasons why.

At this point in the Value Innovation Process the pair of interviewees are very comfortable with each other. They fully understand how you all arrived at this point. They are about to see the fruits of their labor. There is great anticipation on the interviewees part. Of the three interviews, this one is generally the most satisfying and the one the interviewees enjoy the most. The interviewees who gave you a "3" rating at the end of the first round are likely to give you a 4.5 or 5 at the end of this interview.

Developing the 3rd Round Instrument: In the 3rd Round there are five sections:

Introduction – Background
Review the Top Attributes
Description of the Options with Questions
Selection of the "Top 2" or "Top 3"
Wrap - Up

- **Introduction – Background:**
  - Confirm the objectives for the project
  - Share the outputs from the 2nd Round, e.g., "We have completed six interviews with the same Subject Matter Experts. We revised the Rank Order of the attributes, averaged the values being delivered to you today for each attribute - the "As Is", averaged the value that you want to see in the new product (or service) – the "To Be", modified the metrics and captured the absolute value for each metric. The Top 4 attributes in order of importance, based on your inputs are: __________, __________, __________, and __________.
  - State the objectives for Round 3: e.g., "We plan to share with you the options we have developed to address the top attributes you defined, show you how each option functions, the value we expect to deliver for each of the top attributes and have you critique and rate each option. We will share how each option will be priced and have you select your top 2 or 3 options."

- **Review the Top Attributes (Elements of Performance), their ranking, etc.**

"Recall we reviewed the attributes with you in the second round. You confirmed these were the right attributes. We have listed the "Top 5" in the order of importance you shared with us. This ranking is the average of the inputs from 12 interviewees. Are you comfortable with this list and the rank order?

Attribute	Your Ranking
First Element of Performance	1
Second Element of Performance	2
Third Element of Performance	3
Fourth Element of Performance	4
Fifth Element of Performance	5

If they are comfortable that you have captured the "Top 5" correctly, move on to the options and questions. If not, modify the list and rank order based on their inputs and then move to the options.

- **Description of the Options with Questions:**

We recommend:

- You develop and share at least three options with the interviewees. If you want to do more, be mindful of time. You only have 1 hour. Options encourage more dialogue and you will continue to learn as a result.
- Use a graphic artist or industrial designer to sketch your new product or service. The more realistic the better!
- Use a Likert Scale (1) - 5 point in North America and a 7 point outside North America, see Figure 54, to have the interviewees share their thoughts on how well each option addresses each attribute:

Figure 54: Table set up to capture Interviewee Inputs using a 7 point Likert Scale

Interviewee 1	Very Strongly Agree	Strongly Agree	Agree	Neutral	Disagree	Strongly Disagree	Very Strongly Disagree
Deliver equivalent, or better ________							
Increase success rates from ________							
Reduce times by ________							

Interviewee 2	Very Strongly Agree	Strongly Agree	Agree	Neutral	Disagree	Strongly Disagree	Very Strongly Disagree
Deliver equivalent, or better ________							
Increase success rates from ________							
Reduce times by ________							

This will give you an average rating for each option from the 12 interviewees. If you have a situation where you are interviewing people in both Europe and North America, use the appropriate scale and scoring approach provided in Figure 55.

Table 55: Scoring using a Likert Scale for inputs from both Europe (EU) and North America (NA)

Score for	Very Strongly Disagree	Strongly Disagree	Disagree	Neutral	Agree	Strongly Agree	Very Strongly Agree
EU	0	1	2	3	4	5	6
NA	Not used	1	2	3	4	5	Not used

- **Selection of the "Top 2 or 3"**

At this point you need to make a decision on whether you want to share pricing, or price range for each option with the interviewees. If you elect to provide pricing, present that information in the form of a table. If you elect not to share pricing, you should consider asking them, "What would you be prepared to pay for each option?" Typically they will come back with answers like, "I'd be prepared to pay more than we do today because ......, or, "I would not want to pay anymore, but we would make you our preferred supplier."

Here are the questions you will use:

1. Based on the options we have shared with you, if you could only pick one, which would it be and why?
2. If you could have a second choice, which one would it be and why?

	Preferred Option	Second Choice
Interviewee #1		
Interviewee #2		

- **Wrap Up.** This includes:
  - An evaluation of the value of the three rounds of interviews to them (on a 1-5 scale (1 = Low Value; 5 = Exceptional Value)
    In our experience the lowest rating you will receive at this point is a 4.
  - What they enjoyed most about the process?

    You will hear comments like this:

    "It was great to have a second person with me on the interview. Their thinking really helped me. It also kept my answers in check because I knew there was another subject matter expert on the call."

    "Wow."

    "I reflect back on what we've been through and I have learned more about what I do. The process has helped me."

    "I cannot wait to get my hands on this new product."

    "I cannot wait to start using this new service"

    "Great job! Thank You"
  - What they liked the least about the process?

    At this point, there is generally very little that comes up. They may say that the 2nd Round interview was not as exciting as the 1st and 3rd Round interviews.
  - Would they be willing to participate on a future project?

You will find this is an overwhelming "Yes"

At the very end take this opportunity to thank them for the outstanding job they have done (Give them all 6's) and share when and how the gift, gift card, or honorarium will be sent to them.

Output from the 3rd Round Interview:

The output from the 3rd Round is the interviewees preferred option on "How" you can deliver the "What" defined in the "To Be" Value Curve with Metrics.

You have completed the 10-Step Value Innovation Process and are now in a position to make a "Go/No Go" decision on whether this becomes a full-fledged project. If you have come this far, we would expect it will be a "Go" because you will be delivering exceptional value to your Most Important Customer with this new product or service.

Next Steps:

1. Develop the 3rd round instrument
2. Conduct all six interviews.
3. Analyze the outputs:
    - Summarize the rankings for the Options you presented
    - Identify the preferred option
4. Store all documents generated in data central.
5. You have now completed the 10-Step Value Innovation Process. Congratulations!

Takeaways:

1. The 12 interviewees will enjoy this 3rd and final Round interview.
2. You will have a high degree of confidence in how this new product or service will perform in the marketplace.
3. You will know what issues need to be addressed very early on if this effort becomes a full-fledged product
4. If you do not have the technology in your organization to commercialize this new offering, you know exactly what you need and can give clear instructions to those in your Open Innovation group to in-source that technology

Chapter 11

"Wrap Up and Next Steps"

"The cure for Apple is not cost-cutting. The cure for Apple is to innovate its way out of its current predicament."

Steve Jobs, Apple

"Steve, thank you for being a mentor and a friend. Thanks for showing that what you build can change the world. I will miss you."

"When you give everyone a voice and give people power, the system usually ends up in a really good place. So, what we view our role as, is giving people that power."

Mark Zuckerberg, Facebook

"My main job was developing talent. I was a gardener providing water and other nourishment to our top 750 people. Of course, I had to pull out some weeds, too."

"Willingness to change is a strength, even if it means plunging part of the company into total confusion for a while."

Jack Welch, GE

John Doerr, a partner with Kleiner Perkins Caufield & Byers, hosted a dinner at his Silicon Valley home February, 2011. Figure 56 gives you a snapshot of the attendees at this unique event.

Figure 56: The World's Richest Dinner Party "Between us, we're worth $1 trillion"

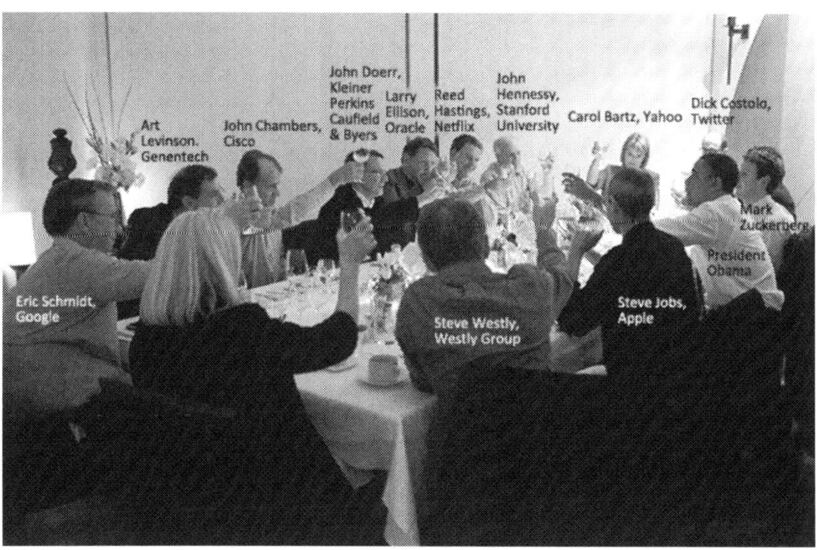

Let's raise our glasses to Value Innovation Works. Wouldn't that have been a great toast!

We have defined the Value Innovation Process, we have walked you through the ten steps of that Process and we have shown you how to use the enabling tools.

It is time for you to make a decision. "We have to adopt this process", or, "No thank you", or "something in between". If you vote "Thumbs Up", on the Value Innovation Process, what are your next steps? "What do I do and how do I do it?" The answer depends on where you are in your organization. Figure 57 provides ideas on how to move forward.

Figure 57: Options on "How" to implement the Value Innovation Process in your organization

Your Position	Actions you Take – Setting the Stage	How to recognize and address the Pitfalls and Culture
CEO, Managing Director or Business Unit Head	You are in a unique position. You alone can decide that your business will use the Value Innovation Process and tools. If your company makes decisions on a consensus basis, you need to sell your direct reports.	The Corporate Immune System will push back on the adoption of the Value Innovation Process.
"C" level or VP Level	You are also well positioned to drive this. Maximize the chances of	

	success by: ➢ Being the Champion of the process ➢ Requiring a significant percentage of associates be trained ➢ Attending a 2- or 3-Day Workshop yourself...this sends a huge positive message and will be worth it, even if you feel you cannot spend back to back days. ➢ Appoint a Value Innovation Process Manager ➢ Talk about Value Innovation every time you are in front of the troops. Showcase the successes. ➢ Work on collaboration between the functional areas – breakdown the silos.	Counter it by: ➢ Racking up short term successes ➢ Making sure your project leaders are your best performer s ➢ Project leaders are empowere d and have the resources to get the job done.
Director and Manager Level	It is unlikely that you will be able to drive the adoption of the Value Innovation Process and enabling tools on your own. Here are some	You are bringing a new process and set of

	suggestions for you to consider: ➢ Call your peers in other companies and see what their experience has been. ➢ Develop a game plan to sell your organization. Get your peers to help you' ➢ Meet with your boss and share what you have learned and how you think this could be implemented. Be prepared to answer his/her questions. ➢ Convince your boss to support adoption. ➢ Attend a 2- or 3- Day Value Innovation Workshop and bring your boss with you.	enabling tools into your organization. NIH and the corporate immune system will move to strike it down. Fact and logic will be challenged by politics and emotion based decision making.

Following are the Takeaways from the first ten chapters in this book. Use this as a checklist to help you and your organization implement a Value Innovation Process:

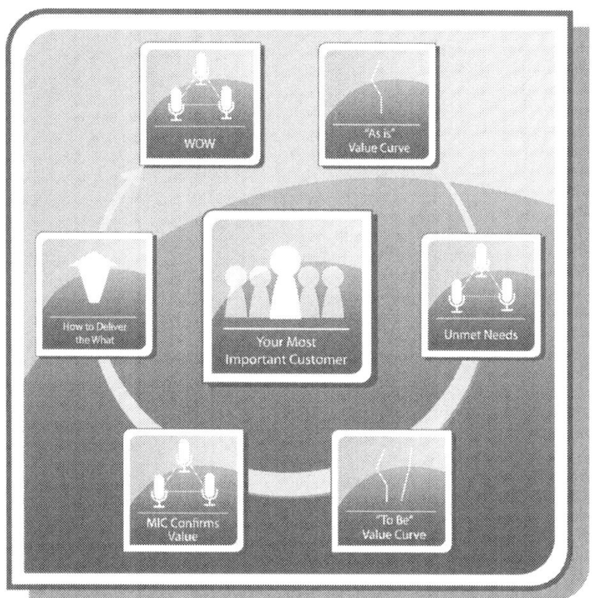

1. The CEO/Managing Director/Business Unit head is the Value Innovation champion driving sustainable, profitable growth.

2. Your company needs:

    - A definition of innovation that everyone in your company understands
    - At least one innovation goal
    - A clear definition of, and support for, Value Innovation across your organization.
    - To train associates on how to Value Innovate.

3. Each function in your organization is responsible for Value Innovation.

4. To keep focus and retain momentum, make decisions quickly and reduce cycle times.

5. Reduce individual workloads when you adopt, install and use the Value Innovation Process.

6. Successful adoption of the Value Innovation Process and enabling tools will drive sustainable, profitable growth.

7. Important trumps Urgent.

Step 1

Define overall project goals and objectives

1. Make sure the project in the Value Innovation Process has a definition consistent with the project. If the definition no longer makes sense, kill the project and start a new one or refine the definition.

2. The project you are going to run through the Value Innovation Process must be defined as well as all the projects you have in your project portfolio.

3. Make sure "What is in Scope" and "What is Out of Scope" is clearly defined and understood by the project team.

Step 2

Develop the Value Chain/Value Web and Identify the Most Important Customer:

1. Develop a Value Chain/Value Web.

2. Use The Three Questions and The Three Questions Template to identify the Most Important Customers in the Value Chain/Value Web.

3. If it is not clear who the Most Important Customer is, there are possibly two Most Important Customers, treat both as Most Important Customers.

4. In the world of B2B, our experience is that most of the time the direct customer is NOT the Most Important Customer.

5. Even in the world of B2C, most large companies will have to deal with an intermediary, e.g., The FMPGCs with mass merchandisers, supermarkets, and other retailers. If you sell directly to the consumer, i.e., you own your own store, restaurant, or lemonade stand, then you are a true B2C business.

6. When the Most Important Customer is identified, it is important to determine the specific person within the company who is the Most Important Customer. Use The Three Questions to identify the Most Important Customer within the Most Important Customer.

7. If you have identified Purchasing or Strategic Sourcing as your Most Important Customer, start this process again. Your target is the entity that is focused on the value you can help bring to their Most Important Customer(s).

8. This process works very well even if your Most Important Customers are inside your organization.

9. If you are a Not-For-Profit you always have two Most Important Customers (One on the donor side and one on the delivery side).

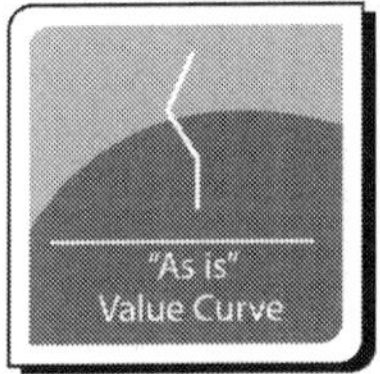

Step 3

Develop "As Is" and "Best in Class" Value Curves with Metrics

1. "As Is" and "Best in Class" Value Curves with Metrics provide a clear picture on the value being delivered to your Most Important Customers for your product or service today.

2. An Element of Performance is a capability or characteristic of your product, service or offering that is important to the Most Important Customer and can be performed/observed in a measurable way.

3. An Element of Performance is succinct. It is not an objective or a feature.

4. Elements of Performance must be measured and rank ordered.

5. There are three ways to develop Elements of Performance:
   - Put yourself in your Most Important Customer's shoes
   - The 7x7 Matrix
   - A combination of both

6. You have three ways to rank order Elements of Performance:
   - User Rank (Easiest to do, takes 5-10 minutes)
   - Pairwise Comparison (Easy to do, takes 15-20 minutes)
   - Analytical Hierarchy Process (Tougher to do, takes 2-3h)

7. Fast Moving Consumer Packaged Goods companies, for both branded and private label products, need to develop Value Curves with Metrics for the Zeroth, First and Second Moments of Truth.

8. Venture capital and equity investors can increase their investment success rates using the Value Innovation Process.

9. You can use Value Curves and Metrics to guide your decisions whether you are a B2B, B2C, B2G or a Not-For-Profit.

10. Technology companies (e.g., Novamin) can significantly benefit using these tools.

11. Not-For-Profits need to develop Value Curves with Metrics for their Most Important Customers on the sponsor and delivery sides of their business.

Step 4

Contextual interview your Most Important Customers to uncover their unmet needs

1. You need to understand the jobs your products and services are hired to do.

2. Marketing has few tools for ferreting out the unarticulated needs of customers.

3. Contextual Interviewing is the most important activity your company can engage in to generate sustainable top line growth. Contextual Interviewing is the single most important activity in the Value Innovation Process. This is the single most important tool you have in the development of new products and services. Get this wrong and everything else in the development cycle will be wrong.

4. The better you plan the interviewing process, the better the results.

5. There are three separate interviews, occurring over a 4 to 6 week period. The goals for the three interviews are different.

6. You will learn more with two interviewees than with one or three interviewees.

7. The interview team must have all key functional areas represented.

8. Selecting your Lead Interviewer is critically important. There are at least two tools to help you make that selection: ISPI or KAI Index.

9. Record all interviews, transcribe them and store them on a server accessible to all project team members.

10. Establish access rights to data central. The future of your company sits in data central.

11. Make these interviews by phone. It is the least expensive, most convenient and least obtrusive way to carry out contextual interviews.

12. It takes a lot of time and effort to do this right. You are mining for gold, it will pay off!

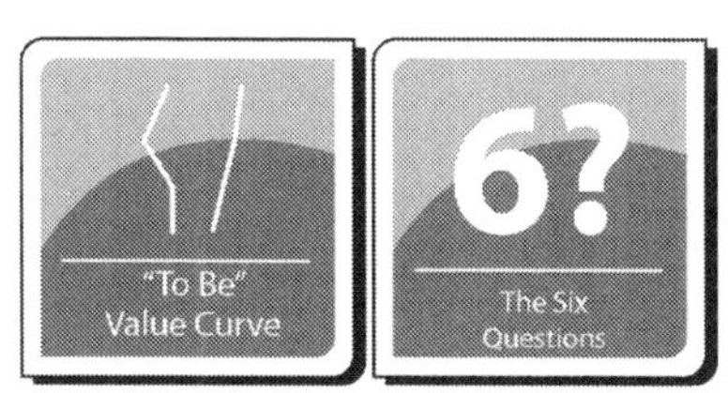

Step 5

Refine the "As Is" and develop the "To Be" Value Curves with Metrics

1. The "As Is" and "To Be" Value Curves with Metrics define what you think you need to do to deliver exceptional value to the Most Important Customer.

2. In the 2nd Round interview (Steps 6 and 7 of the Value Innovation Process), you will have the interviewees critique

the "As Is" and "To Be" Value Curve with Metrics without showing them the Value Curve.

Step 6 & 7

Have the Most Important Customers critique the "As Is' and "To Be" Value Curves with Metrics

1. Steps 6-7 of the Value Innovation Process, the 2nd Round of interviews, will provide you with vetted "As Is" and "To Be" Value Curves with Metrics.

2. "As Is" and "To Be" Value Curves make writing a Value Proposition very easy (Step 8 of the Value Innovation Process).

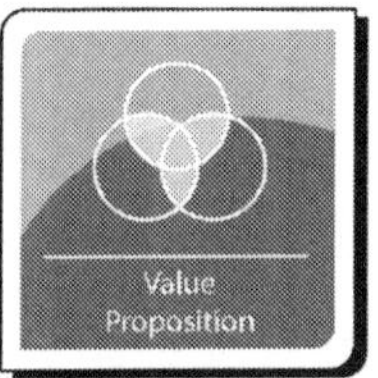

Step 8

Define the Value Proposition

1. With "As Is" and "To Be" Value Curves with metrics in hand, it is easy to write a Value Proposition.

2. Waiting until the value proposition is clearly understood helps you focus on what is truly important and not waste time and energy. Waiting to determine the "How" until step 9 is completed is often difficult for the team. It is human nature to want to solve problems much earlier in the process.

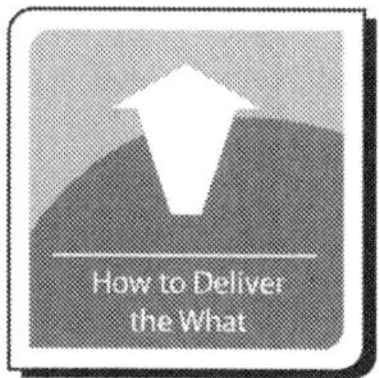

Step 9

Develop options on "How" to deliver the "What"

1. Use TRIZ to identify potential solutions to the problems you need to solve.

2. Use subject matter experts who are not on the project team to develop options on "How to deliver exceptional value to the Most Important Customer".

3. Use accepted brainstorming techniques.

4. Use patent mapping to determine what options you have to develop, buy, or license in technology to develop a unique and defensible position

Step 10

Have the Most Important Customers critique "How" you plan to deliver exceptional value to them

1. The 12 interviewees will enjoy this 3rd and final Round interview.

2. You will have a high degree of confidence in how this new product or service will perform in the marketplace.

3. You will know what issues need to be addressed very early on if this effort becomes a full-fledged product.

4. If you do not have the technology in your organization to commercialize this new offering, you now know exactly what you need. You can give clear instructions to those in your Open Innovation group to in-source that technology.

Our goal in this book has been to raise your level of awareness, excite you about, and sow the seeds of passion for Value Innovation. Our sincere hope is that we have achieved those goals.

The future health of your organization and your country depends on you making Value Innovation Work.

REFERENCES

Chapter 1:

1. Dillon, T., Lee, R.K., & Matheson, D. (2005). Value innovation: Passport to wealth creation. Research*Technology Management, 48(2), 22-36.
2. Smith, L., Goodrich, N. E., Roberts, D., & Scinta, J. (2005). Assessing your organization's potential for value innovation. Research*Technology Management, March-April, 37-42.
3. Balsano, T. J., Goodrich, N. E., Lee, R. K., Miley, J. W., Morse, T. F., & Roberts, D.A. (2008). Identifying your innovation Enablers and Inhibitors, Research*Technology Management, November - December, 51(6), 23-33.
4. Hamel, G. (2000). Reinvent your company – 10 rules for making billion-dollar ideas bubble up from below. Fortune, June 12, 98-118.
5. Hamel, G. (2012). *What Happens Now?* Jossey-Bass, a Wiley Imprint, San Francisco, CA
6. Lafley, A. G. & Charan, R. (2008) *Game-Changer*. New York: Crown Publishing
7. Benner, M. J. (2010). Securities analysts and incumbent response to radical technological change. Academy of Management Journal, 55(1): 213-233.
8. Hill, A. (2012). Kodak in Crisis – Snapshot of a humble giant. Financial Times, April 3, 10
9. Bessant J. & Tidd, J. (2011). *Innovation and Entrepreneurship*. John Wiley and Sons Ltd., Chichester, England.
10. Tidd, J. & Bessant J. (2009). *Managing Innovation: Integrating Technological, Market and Organizational Change*. John Wiley and Sons Ltd., Chichester, England.
11. Von Hippel, E. (1988). *The Sources of Innovation*, Oxford, Oxford University Press.

12. Von Hippel, E. (2005). *Democratizing Innovation.* The MIT Press, Cambridge, MA
13. Von Hippel, E. (2007). Democratizing Innovation Publisher. The MIT Press, Cambridge, MA
14. Christensen, C. (1997). *The Innovator's Dilemma.* Boston: Harvard Business School Publications, Cambridge, MA.
15. Christensen, C. (2003). *The Innovator's Solution: Creating and sustaining successful growth.* Boston: Harvard Business School Publications, Cambridge, MA.
16. Christensen, C., Dyer, J. & Gregerson, H. (2011). *The Innovators' DNA.* Harvard Business School Publications, Cambridge, MA.
17. Hamel, G. (2002). *Leading the Revolution.* New York, NY: Plume a unit of the Penguin Publishing Group.
18. Semler, R. (1995). *Maverick.* Warner Books, NYC, NY.
19. Semler, R. (2004). *The Seven Day Weekend.* The Penguin Group USA, NYC, NY
20. Chesbrough, H. (2006). *Open Innovation – The New Imperative for Creating and Profiting from Technology.* Harvard Business School Publications, Cambridge, MA
21. Chesbrough, H., Vanhaverbeke, W. & West, J. (2006). *Open Innovation – Researching a New Paradigm.* Oxford University Press.
22. Munshi, P. (2009). *Making Breakthrough Innovation Happen – How 11 Indians Pulled Off The Impossible*, Harper Collins, Noida, India.
23. Ulwick, A. W. (2005). *What Customers Want.* The McGraw-Hill Companies, Inc., NYC, NY
24. Leifer, R., McDermott, C.M., O'Connor, G.C., Peters, L.S., Rice, M., & Veryzer, R.W. (2000). Exceptional Growth, Wharton School Publishing, Upper Saddle River, NJ, USA
25. Phillips, J. (2011). *Relentless Innovation*, The McGraw-Hill Companies, Inc., NYC, NY
26. Govindarajan, V. & Trimble, C. (2012). *Reverse Innovation.* Harvard Business School Publications, Cambridde, MA

27. Cooper, R. G. (1988). *Winning at New Products.* Basic Books, NYC, NY
28. Markides, C. (1999). *All the Right Moves*. Boston: Harvard Business School Press, Cambridge, MA.
29. Kim, W.C. & Mauborgne, R. (1997). Value innovation: The strategic logic of high growth. Harvard Business Review, January-February, 103-112.
30. Kim, W.C. & Mauborgne, R. (2005). *Blue Ocean Strategy.* Boston: Harvard Business School Press, Cambridge, MA
31. Miller, W. L. & Morris, L. (1999) 4th Generation R&D. John Wiley and Sons, NYC, NY
32. Prahalad, C.K. & Hamel, G. (1996). *Competing for the future*. Boston: Harvard Business School Publications, Cambridge, MA.
33. Prahalad, C. K. (2009). *The Fortune at the Bottom of the Pyramid.* Prentice Hall, Upper Saddle, NJ
34. Berfield, S. (2010). C. K. Prahalad 1941-2010. BloombergBusinessWeek, April 22.
35. Hamel, G. (1996). Strategy as revolution. Harvard Business Review, July-August, 69-82.
36. Dell, M. (1997). Business Week, October 6.
37. Financial Times, January 26, 2012, p 20 (US edition).
38. Isaacson, W. (2011). Steve Jobs. Simon and Schuster, NYC, NY.
39. Fast Company. (2011) http://www.fastcompany.com/most-innovative-companies/2011/
40. Samsung (2006). BusinessWeek online, June 22.

Chapter 2:

1. Semler R. (1995) *"Maverick: The Success Story behind the World's Most Unusual Workplace,"* Warner Books, New York City, NY.
2. Semler R. (2004) *"The Seven Day Weekend: Changing the Way Work Works,"* Penguin Books, London, England

Chapter 3:

1. Christensen, C. M. and Raynor, M., 2003. "The Innovator's Solution", Harvard Business School Press, pp 116-117.
2. Porter, M. 1985 "Competitive Advantage: Creating and Sustaining Superior Performance." The Free Press, New York, NY.

Chapter 4:

1. Kim, W.C. & Mauborgne, R. (1997). Value innovation: The strategic logic of high growth. Harvard Business Review, January-February, 103-112.
2. Kim, W.C. & Mauborgne, R. (2005). *Blue Ocean Strategy*. Boston: Harvard Business School Press, Cambridge, MA
3. Kim, W. C. and Mauborgne, R. (2002). Charting your company's future. Harvard Business Review, May-June, 77-83.
4. Thurstone, L.L. (1927). A law of comparative judgement. Psychological Review, 34, 278–286
5. Saaty, T. L., Alexander, J. (1989). *Conflict Resolution: The Analytic Hierarchy Process*. Praeger, New York, New York.
6. Ihlwon, M. (2006) Bloomberg BusinessWeek, July 3. http://www.businessweek.com/magazine/content/06_27/b3991052.htm

Chapter 5:

1. Christensen, C., & Raynor, M. (2003). *The Innovator's Solution*. Harvard Business School Press, Cambridge, MA.

2. Kelley, T. & Littman, J. (2001). *The Art of Innovation.* New York, NY: Currency-Doubleday.
3. Kelley, T. & Littman, J. (2005). *The Ten Faces of Innovation.* New York, NY: Currency-Doubleday.
4. Kirton, M.J. (2003). *Adaption-Innovation.* Routledge, London, UK.
5. Rosenfeld, R. (2011). http://www.innovating.com/innovation-strengths-preference-indicator/
6. Gitomer, J. (2007). *Little Green Book of Getting Your Way.* FT Press, London, UK.
7. Whitney, J. (1996). "Strategic Renewal for Business Units," Harvard Business Review, July-August, 84-98.
8. Katz, G. (2011). "Nine myths about the Voice of the Customer," PDMA Visions, October, Chicago, IL, USA.

Chapter 6:

1. Unknown Author. (2006). http://images.businessweek.com/ss/06/06/samsung/index_01.htm
2. Ihlwon, M. (2006) Bloomberg BusinessWeek, July 3. http://www.businessweek.com/magazine/content/06_27/b3991052.htm

Chapter 9:

1. Osborn, A.F. (1963). *Applied imagination: Principles and procedures of creative problem solving* (Third Revised Edition). New York, NY: Charles Scribner's Sons.
2. De Bono, E. (1999). *Six Thinking Hats.* Boston: Back Bay Books (First published in 1985).

Chapter 10:

1. Likert, R. (1932). "A Technique for the Measurement of Attitudes". Archives of Psychology **140**: 1–55.

Glossary of Terms

Term	Definition
4th Generation R&D	Primary Proponents: William L. Miller and Langdon Morris Describes the transition to new ways of doing business in a knowledge-based economy that offers new learning opportunities for individuals and new ways to achieve more agile resource deployment throughout society
Analytical Hierarchy Process (AHP)	Is a structured technique for organizing and analyzing complex decisions. Based on mathematics and psychology, it was developed by Thomas L. Saaty in the 1970s and has been extensively studied and refined since then (Reference). It is a more rigorous and refined process than Pairwise Comparison but it takes much longer to do than Pairwise Comparison. If you were to rank order ten Elements with a group of four or five people, the process could take 2 to 3 hours.
Anthropology	The science of human beings; *especially* **:** the study of human beings and their ancestors through time and space and in relation to physical character, environmental and social relations, and culture the science of human beings;
"As Is"	This is a curve in the Value Curve with Metrics that addresses the current state – the value you are delivering, or competitors, are delivering for each Element of Performance in the Value Curve with Metrics
"Best in Class"	The product or service that delivers the highest value to the Most Important Customer for that

	Element of Performance. A Value Curve with Metrics has multiple Elements of Performance, hence the "Best in Class" value Curve may be made up by several products and services. "Best in Class" probably doesn't exist in one product or service. Exceptions: RE/MAX International and Carbon Motors E-7 police car.
B2C	A company that sells directly to the consumer. It also is used to define companies in the fast moving consumer packaged goods business who sell to mass merchants and supermarkets, who in turn sell to the consumer
B2B	A company that sells it products and services to another business
B2G	A company that sells its products and services to the Federal, State or Local government
Brainstorming	Osborn had his four general rules of brainstorming, established with intention to reduce social inhibitions among group members, stimulate idea generation, and increase overall creativity of the group. 1. **Focus on quantity:** This rule is a means of enhancing divergent production, aiming to facilitate problem solving through the maxim quantity breeds quality. The assumption is that the greater the number of ideas generated, the greater the chance of producing a radical and effective solution. 2. **Withhold criticism:** In brainstorming, criticism of ideas generated should be put 'on hold'. Instead, participants should focus on extending or adding to ideas, reserving criticism for a later 'critical stage' of the process. By suspending judgment, participants will feel free to generate unusual ideas.

	3. **Welcome unusual ideas:** To get a good and long list of ideas, unusual ideas are welcomed. They can be generated by looking from new perspectives and suspending assumptions. These new ways of thinking may provide better solutions. 4. **Combine and improve ideas:** Good ideas may be combined to form a single better good idea, as suggested by the slogan "1+1=3". It is believed to stimulate the building of ideas by a process of association. Procter and Gamble has formalized this process with their MIB (Make It Bigger) Meetings. Osborn notes that brainstorming should address a specific question. By focusing on the "As Is" and "To Be" Value Curves with Metrics, you are doing exactly that. He held that sessions addressing multiple questions were inefficient.
CPG	Consumer Packaged Goods
Classical Innovation	Primary Proponents: John Bessant (University of Exeter, UK) and Joe Tidd (University of Sussex) Links business strategy with innovation strategy and focuses on innovation and entpreneurship. Based on a very simplistic four step process: Recognize Opportunity, Find Resources, Develop Venture, Create Value
Contextual Interviewing	A process to uncover the unmet, unarticulated needs of your Most Important Customers. There are three interviews, each 1h in length, carried out at different times with an interview team and 2 Most Important Customers. The interviews each have a different focus: Divergent (Listening); Convergent (Shaping)

	and Convergent (Defining)
Customer Centric Innovation	Primary Proponent: Eric von Hippel (MIT) Innovation that focuses on the customer for the product or service
Delphi Method	Experts answer questionnaires, or address questions, in two or more rounds. After each round, a facilitator provides an anonymous summary of the experts' forecasts from the previous round as well as the reasons they provided for their judgments. Thus, experts are encouraged to revise their earlier answers in light of the replies of other members of their panel. It is believed that during this process the range of the answers will decrease and the group will converge towards the "correct" answer. Finally, the process is stopped after a pre-defined stop criterion (e.g. number of rounds, achievement of consensus, stability of results) and the mean or median scores of the final rounds determine the results. This process can be used by a project team to rank order Elements of Performance.
Disruptive Innovation	Primary Proponent: Clayton Christenson (Harvard) A new technology that enables higher value solutions to a customer group's problems and disrupts the existing marketplace
EPS	Earnings per share. The portion of a company's profit allocated to each outstanding share of common stock. Earnings per share serves as an indicator of a company's profitability. Read more: http://www.investopedia.com/terms/e/eps.asp#ixzz1tBvzhSWP
Element of	An Element of Performance is a capability or characteristic of your product, service or offering

Performance	that is important to the Most Important Customer and can be performed/observed in a measurable way. Reference, Steve Scacher, EPMO, Chevron. An Element of Performance is a succinct statement. It is not an objective, nor is it a feature/benefit, e.g., We are a Belgian brewery developing a new beer. One of the Elements of Performance is very likely to be Taste. It is not, Improve Taste – this is an objective. It is not Tastes Great – this is a feature. The "To Be" and "As Is" Value Curves with Metrics will tell us what we need to do with taste to deliver greater value to the consumer.
FMCPG	Fast Moving Consumer Packaged Goods
First Moment of Truth (FMOT)	Ms. Consumer determines she will buy the product based on what she sees and reads on the package. Feel of the package may play a role also (This is especially true for products like toilet paper and face tissue). Winning the First Moment of Truth with the first time buyer is the first step a FMCPG company takes in growing market share
GoToWebinar	Provides web conferencing and online meeting tools. Web-based services for everything from online meetings to remote support and file storage. An operating unit of Citrix.http://www.gotomeeting.com/fec/
Innovation	Innovation is the creation of better or more effective products, processes, services, technologies, or ideas that are accepted by markets, governments, and society. Innovation differs from invention in that innovation refers to the use of a new idea or method, whereas invention refers more directly to the creation of the idea or method itself. Source: Wikipedia.

Intellectual Assets	Intellectual Assets Corp., headquartered in the San Francisco Bay area, is a professional advisory services firm specializing in integrated business, R&D, and IP processes. Intellectual Assets, Inc. is distinguished by using cutting edge IP assessment tools and proprietary software. The company also offers invaluable insights based on the depth and breadth of executive level management experience and industry coverage the firm's members represent.
In scope	The work that needs to be accomplished to deliver a product, service, or result with the specified features and functions
ISPI	The ISPI® highlights 12 orientations that compose an individual's predispositions for a certain type of innovation. It makes visible the way an individual prefers to solve problems and what impacts their motivation, passion and decision-making. The ISPI® also shows how one prefers to work with others and deal with control. These orientations impact innovation results. ISPI was developed by Dr Robert Rosenfeld of Idea Connection Systems. http://www.innovating.com/
KAI Index	The Kirton Adaptor Innovation Index developed by Dr Michael J Kirton. Michael Kirton is director and founder of the Occupational Research Centre. He is the originator of the Adaption-Innovation Theory and Inventory (KAI). .KAI Index is determined using a 33 Item Instrument and can be completed in 15 minutes.
Likert Scale	Is a psychometric scale commonly involved in research that employs questionnaires. It is the most widely used approach to scaling responses in survey research, such that the term is often used interchangeably with rating scale, or more

	accurately the Likert-type scale, even though the two are not synonymous. The scale is named after its inventor, psychologist Source: Wikipedia
Management Innovation	Primary Proponent: Gary Hamel (The Management Lab) Establishes "Ten Rules" for bubbling up billion dollar ideas. [These "Ten Rules" were the foundation of the Ten Principles used to develop the Value IQ Instrument by RoR 99-7 {VI-I} at the Industrial Research Institute
Most Important Customer	Once you have developed your value Chain or Value Web, you use the 3 Questions and the Three Question Template to identify the Most Important Customer and any key Influencers. It is important to understand that the Most Important Customer could be the user of your product or service, they may not buy it, or sell it.
NPV	Net present value. The difference between the present value of cash inflows and the present value of cash outflows. NPV is used in capital budgeting to analyze the profitability of an investment or project. Read more: http://www.investopedia.com/terms/n/npv.asp#ixzz1tBxgrTiz
Not-For-Profit	A Not-For-Profit organization is neither a legal nor technical definition but generally refers to an organization that uses surplus revenues to achieve its goals rather than to distribute them as profit or dividends. States in the United States defer to the IRS designation conferred under United States Internal Revenue Code Section 501©, when the IRS deems an organization eligible. They may or may not have shareholders.
Open	Primary Proponent: Henry Chesbrough (UC

Innovation	Berkeley) Innovation efforts extend beyond the organization reaching out to SME's, Universities, members of the public, etc.
Orbit Shifting Innovation	Primary Proponents: Rajiv Narang (Erewhon) and Bhupendra Sharma (NXTLYF) The NexGen Stage-Gate Process. Addresses cultural barriers and stakeholder behavior before working on the process
Out of scope	Increase or decrease in the scope of work that is considered outside the statement of work on which a project is based.
Outcome Driven Innovation	Primary Proponent: Tony Ulwick (Strategyn) An 8-step innovation methodology is focused on devising and positioning solutions that address unmet customer needs. Steps 1-5 are dedicated to identifying hidden opportunities that exist in new or existing markets. Steps 6-8 focus on using those insights to leverage advantages of current products
Pairwise Comparison	Pairwise Comparison refers to any process of comparing Elements of Performance in pairs to judge which of each Element is preferred by the Most Important Customer. (Reference- L. L. Thurstone first introduced a scientific approach to using pairwise comparisons for measurement in 1927 Wikipedia)
Patent Mapping	A patent map provides a snapshot of the overall IP landscape by plotting every patent in the field on a map. It looks just like a topology map.
ROI	Return on Investment (not Innovation). A performance measure used to evaluate the efficiency of an investment or to compare the efficiency of a number of different investments.

	To calculate ROI, the benefit (return) of an investment is divided by the cost of the investment; the result is expressed as a percentage or a ratio. Read more: http://www.investopedia.com/terms/r/returnoninvestment.asp#ixzz1tBwzmiW8
Radical Innovation	Primary Proponents: Mark Rice (Bentley) and Gina O'Connor (RPI) How traditional corporations build the radical, innovative capabilities of start-ups. Defines the new managerial competencies firms will need in order to outsmart upstart challengers and the patterns through which game-changing innovation occurs in established companies
Rank Ordering	Tools used to determine which Element of Performance is the most important to the Most Important Customer, the next most important, and so on. There are three rank ordering tools: Analytical Hierarchy Process, Pairwise Comparison and User Rank
ReadyTalk	A privately held company headquartered in Denver, CO that provides the following services: Web Conferencing Audio Conferencing Webinars & Services Recording & Syndication Integrations http://www.readytalk.com/
Reinvention Workshop	As Alcan moved into Step 9 of the Value Innovation Process they decided to involve the pharmaceutical company in the process through a Reinvention Workshop. We think this was a first. The goal: Immerse them in the Value

	Innovation Process and win their "buy-in."
Relentless Innovation	Primary Proponent: Jeffrey Phillips (OVO/NetCentrics) Organizations need to make innovation Business As Usual and empower middle managers
Reverse Innovation	Primary Proponents: C. K. Prahalad, Vijay Govindarajan and Chris Trimble Calls for a much greater recognition of the developing world. What can a company in the G20 do to penetrate new, high growth markets where GDP/capita is low? How could these same companies take advantage of importing new products and services from these countries into their home market.
Second Moment of Truth (SMOT)	Ms. Consumer opens the product, uses it at home and is delighted by how the product performs
Slalom®	A software package that uses .xlsm templates and algorithms to generate Value Curves with Metrics. Allows the user to rank order Elements of Performance using three different methods, define Element metrics and more.
Stage-Gate Innovation	Primary Proponents: Bob Cooper and Scott Edgett (Product Development Institute) Disciplined process to move from ideation to commercialization
Strategic Innovation	Primary Proponent: Constantinos Markides (London Business School) A fundamental reconceptualization of what the business is about, which in turn leads to a dramatically different way of playing the game in

	industry. How firms must rewire their "organizational DNA across structure, staffing, systems and culture
Strategy Canvas	The strategy canvas is the central diagnostic and action framework for building a compelling blue ocean strategy. The horizontal axis captures the range of factors that the industry competes on and invests in, and the vertical axis captures the offering level that buyers receive across all these key competing factors.
Supply Chain	Supply chain management (SCM) is the management of a network of interconnected businesses involved in the ultimate provision of product and service packages required by end customers. Supply chain management spans all movement and storage of raw materials, work-in-process inventory, and finished goods from point of origin to point of consumption - Wikipedia
"To Be"	This is a curve in the Value Curve with Metrics that addresses the future state. Based on inputs from the 1st Round of Contextual Interviews and the 6 Questions, the "To Be" Value Curve defines what value must be delivered to the Most Important Customer.
The Six Questions	Used to develop the "To Be" Value Curve 7. What element of performance or service should we decrease the value delivered or even eliminate? 8. What element of performance or service should we increase the value delivered? 9. What new element of performance or service could we introduce that has not been thought of before? 10. Do these changes make the value proposition for the Most Important Customer compelling?

	11. Is this position unique? 12. Do we need to, can we defend this position?
The Three Questions	The three questions are used with the Value Chain or Value Web to identify the Most Important Customer. They are: 6. If there's a problem with your product, service, or offering, who is responsible for fixing it? 7. If there's a problem with your product, service or offering, who stands to lose the most financially? 8. Who sees the value?
The Three Question Template	Combines the Value Chain or Value Web with the Three Questions. By completing the template you identify the Most Important Customer(s)
Unarticulated Needs	The Most Important Customer is not able to succinctly describe what they need. "Asking them what they need" leads to an unplanned, poorly thought through response. Typically these kinds of response are brought back by the sales force and waste countless resources in R&D, engineering and marketing. Unarticulated needs are surfaced using a set of open ended questions to uncover problems that the Most Important Customer is experiencing, or expects to experience.
Unmet Needs	Needs that the Most Important Customer has that are not being met. E.g., Most major airlines do not provide WiFi on every flight and do not have power outlets at each seat. The business traveler needs both. When he/she flies Virgin America his/her needs are met.
TRIZ	TRIZ (pronounced TREEZ) is the Russian acronym for the Theory of Inventive Problem Solving. This proven algorithmic approach to solving technical problems began in 1946 when the Russian engineer and scientist Genrikh

	Altshuller studied thousands of patents and noticed certain patterns. From these patterns he discovered that the evolution of a technical system is not a random process, but is governed by certain objective laws. These laws can be used to consciously develop a system along its path of technical evolution - by determining and implementing innovations. One result of Altshuller's theory -- that inventiveness and creativity can be learned -- has fundamentally altered the psychological model of creativity.
Value Chain	The Value Chain identifies each company, organization, or individual involved in a buying, selling, or using transaction between you and the ultimate end user. The Value Chain/Value Web begins where your product or service begins its' life. The Value Chain/Value Web ends the when the product is finally used.
Value Curve with Metrics	Provides you with a clear snapshot of your project. It's divided into two halves. The left side of the Value Curve lists the Elements of Performance in order of importance to the Most Important Customer. The first Element is the most important to the Most Important Customer. In aggregate these Elements define your product, service or offering. The right side lists both values being delivered to the Most Important Customer for your current offering ("As Is" - if you have one) and "Best in Class" on a value scale (low on the left and high on the right). Each Element has a value.
Value Innovation	Primary Proponents: W Chan Kim, Renee Mauborgne (INSEAD)

	Richard K. Lee (Value Innovations, Inc.) Delivering Exceptional Value to the Most Important Customer in the Value Chain, all the time, every time.
Value Proposition	The Value Proposition succinctly describes how your product or service will deliver exceptional value to your Most Important Customer(s). The "As Is" and "To Be" Value Curves with Metrics help you define what you are going to do to deliver exceptional value to the Most Important Customer.
Value Web	Like the Value Chain, the Value Web identifies each company, organization, or individual involved in a buying, selling, or using the transaction between you and the ultimate end user.
VerbaLink	A transcription service based in Santa Monica, CA. Using court reporters they will transcribe a 1h recored interview in less than 48h. Price is approximately $250/transcript http://www.verbalink.com/
Webex	WebEx Communications Inc. is a Cisco company that provides on-demand collaboration, online meeting, web conferencing and videoconferencing applications. Its products include Meeting Center, Training Center, Event Center, Support Center, Sales Center, MeetMeNow, PCNow, WebEx AIM Pro Business Edition, WebEx WebOffice, and WebEx Connect. http://www.webex.com/
Whitney's Rules	20% of your customers generate 80% of your profits. You can characterize your customers

	using three questions: Is your customer strategically significant in their market(s)? Yes or No Does your customer buy a lot of your products and services? Yes or No Do you deliver strong margins off your business with this customer? Yes or No This results in 8 different customer classes
Zeroth Moment of Truth (ZMOT)	The company has delivered consistent and meaningful value to Ms Consumer in the products she uses from the company, so she is willing to try a new product manufactured and marketed by that same company. FMCPG companies must win a significant percentage of ZMOTs with every new product introduction.

INDEX

ABOUT THE AUTHORS

Richard ("Dick") K. Lee

Dick is CEO and Chief Innovation Officer of Value Innovations, Inc. Value Innovations, incorporated as a Chapter C Corporation in Colorado in August, 1999, helps its customers significantly improve the contribution of new products, services and delivery to their company's value by providing exceptional value to the most important customer in the value chain. He is a black belt in Value Innovation.

Dick has managed, and had full P&L responsibility for operating units of Fortune 500 Companies and led R&D organizations. He served as Vice President, Strategic Business Operations, Johns Manville Corporation; Vice President R&D

for Pharmaseal, a division of American Hospital Supply and subsequently Baxter Healthcare Corporation; Vice President, Onan Corporation and General Manager, Elgar Corporation (McGraw Edison Corporation); Vice President and General Manager, the Portable Battery Division of Gould Inc.; and Manager, Vehicle Emission Control R&D, UOP Inc. He started his career as a research chemist at UOP.

Since 1992, Value Innovations has delivered >100 workshops and webinars to >300 clients and Dick has led consulting projects for clients in North America and Europe, including: ADM, Albany International, American Vanguard, Ashland Chemical, Associated Octel, AstenJohnson, Bobcat, Caterpillar Trimble Control Technologies, Cargill, Champion Technologies, Chevron, Ciba Corning Diagnostics, Ciba Geigy, ECC Inc., Exxon Research and Engineering, Gates Corporation, Genencor, Goodyear Tire and Rubber Company, Great Lakes Chemical Corporation, Hussmann, Honeywell, Ingersoll-Rand, Johns Manville, Johnson Controls, KBR (an operating unit of Halliburton), Kennametal, Merck KGaA, Millipore, Mobil Oil Corporation, Nanophase, Novamin (acquired by GlaxoSmithKline in 2009), PG&E, Philip Morris USA, Polycore USA, Procter and Gamble, Raychem, SAIC, Sherwin Williams, and Thermo King.

The primary areas of focus for the consulting projects have been: strategic business, technology and innovation planning; value innovation; development of growth strategies; bench marking; contextual interviewing; technology outsourcing; facilitation of steering teams; the development of custom Stage-Gate project management systems; and portfolio management.

Dick was Chairman of the Organizing Committee for Summit 91, for which he authored a widely distributed 30-minute videotape entitled; U.S. Competitiveness: – a Crisis! – continuing as a member of the Summit 92 organizing committee. Focused on improving U.S. competitiveness, Summit 91 brought together leaders from industry, academia (Lester Thurow, MIT; George Cabot Lodge and Bruce Scott, Harvard Business School), government (then HUD Secretary,

Jack Kemp), and other key players (Clyde Prestowitz, President of the Economic Strategy Institute, and Kent Hughes, President of the Council on Competitiveness).

Dick is a past Member of the Board of Directors, Industrial Research Institute (IRI). Dick was a member of the European Industrial Research Management Association's Working Group 61, "Organizing Stage-Gate to Deliver Value". Dick co-chaired the RoR Subcommittee, "Value Creation through Value Innovation" with Tom Dillon, Senior Group VP at SAIC, from 1999-2002. Nina Goodrich was a key member of this team. This subcommittee, represented by over forty IRI member companies, developed the first value innovation process and the Value IQ Tool (now called VIPAT – Value Innovation Process Assessment Tool). Nina had VIPAT translated into Spanish, German and French.

Dick served as Vice Chairman of the Rocky Mountain World Trade Center; member of its Board of Directors and Executive Committee; Chairman of the Trade & Business Policy Committee, and led a group of volunteers that developed "An Export Growth Goal Plan for the State of Colorado".

Dick has a BS degree from the University of London and was awarded a Fulbright Travel Scholarship. He has an MS from Northwestern University, and earned a Ph.D. in inorganic chemistry from the University of London. Dick completed the Mini MBA program at the College of St. Thomas. He is cited in Who's Who in America (1992 - present), Who's Who Worldwide, and is a winner of an IR-100 Award (Zinc/Air Hearing Aid Button Cells).

Dick is networked at the first level to >1,700 business professionals on LinkedIn providing him with access to >12 million professionals on LinkedIn through his network.

Dick is a UK subject and a Permanent Resident of the US. He has traveled frequently to Europe and The Far East. A resident of Castle Pines, Dick enjoys golf and skiing with his wife Lin. Their daughters, Sonja and Alyssa, are married with two sons each and live in the greater Denver Metro Area.

Nina E. Goodrich

Nina is the Principal at Sustainnovation Solutions, a consultancy combining innovation and sustainability. She strongly believes that innovation and sustainability are linked as key drivers for future growth and value. Nina has combined her extensive background in R & D and innovation with sustainability to create a platform for opportunity.

Nina has been a student of the innovation process for many years, and an advocate for innovation throughout business organizations. Nina is a black belt in Value Innovation.

Nina and Dick share a passion for Value Innovation and have worked together first through co-chairing working groups at the Industrial Research Institute (IRI) and later developing and implementing Value Innovation programs with industry. Their collaboration started with the development of a tool to measure an organization's culture for innovation. At the time Nina was the Director of Innovation for Alcan Global

Pharmaceutical Packaging. She used the tool to measure Alcan's innovation culture, benchmarked it against other IRI companies and developed interventions to enhance the innovation culture. It became obvious that the development of an internal Value Innovation Process was critical.

At Alcan her responsibilities included developing the Alcan Packaging front end of innovation process. As Value Innovation Champion, Nina created a variety of internal and external workshops using Value Curves with Metrics, Value Chains, Value Webs and stakeholder maps to guide the front end of innovation. She created strategies to teach and implement these concepts internally and collaboratively with customers. The Reinvention Workshop was a major hit.

As a lifetime student of the innovation process Nina has developed a number of technology plans in many industries to help organizations answer the mandate of growth through innovation. She knows first-hand how easy it is to articulate and how difficult it is to execute. Nina has held the following technology management positions: Alcan Packaging - Director, Sustainnovation; Alcan Global Pharmaceutical Packaging - Director, Innovation; Amcor PET Packaging - Director, Value Creation and Business Innovation and Guelph Food Technology Centre - Director Operations.

Nina has pursued graduate work in technology management and has a BA in Molecular Biology from Wellesley College in Massachusetts.

She is a frequent speaker at industry events and has many publications.

Made in the USA
Charleston, SC
25 November 2013